# MINDFULNESS
# AND MONEY

# MINDFULNESS AND MONEY

## The Buddhist Path of Abundance

### Kulananda and Dominic Houlder

BROADWAY BOOKS · NEW YORK

BROADWAY

Broadway Books titles may be purchased for business or promotional use or for special sales. For information, please write to: Special Markets Department, Random House, Inc., 280 Park Avenue, New York, NY 10017.

"The Parable of Medicinal Herbs" on pages 62–63 from *The Lotus Sutra,* translated by Burton Watson. Copyright © 1993 Columbia University Press. Reprinted with the permission of the publisher.
"Health is the highest gain, contentment the greatest riches" on page 130 reproduced from *Dhammapada: The Way of Truth,* translated by Sangharakshita, Windhorse Publications, Birmingham, England, 2001.
"If you speak the truth, . . . of your own hearts" on pages 158–59 from *One Robe, One Bowl: The Zen Poetry of Ryokan,* translated by John Stevens. Copyright © 1977 Weatherhill, Inc. Reprinted with the permission of the publisher.
Dr. Santorelli's story and "21 Ways to Be Mindful" on pages 197 through 201 reproduced from *Mindfulness and Meaningful Work: Explorations in Right Livelihood* by Claude Whitmeyer with permission of Parallax Press, Berkeley, California.

PRINTED IN THE UNITED STATES OF AMERICA

BROADWAY BOOKS and its logo, a letter B bisected on the diagonal, are trademarks of Broadway Books, a division of Random House, Inc.

Visit our website at www.broadwaybooks.com

First edition published 2002

Book design by Caroline Cunningham

Library of Congress Cataloging-in-Publication Data
Kulananda.
Mindfulness and money : the Buddhist path of abundance / Kulananda and Dominic Houlder.—1st ed.
p. cm.
1. Wealth—Religious aspects—Buddhism. 2. Finance, Personal—Moral and ethical aspects. 3. Rich people—Conduct of life. 4. Five Precepts (Buddhism). 5. Buddhism—Doctrines. I. Houlder, Dominic. II. Title.
BQ4570.W4 K85 2002
294.3'568—dc21
2002025863

ISBN 0-7679-0914-3

1  3  5  7  9  10  8  6  4  2

# Contents

▾  v  ▾

## PART TWO

# The Path of Abundance

# Preface

Let us briefly introduce ourselves. The two writers of this book live apparently very different lives. Kulananda lives in a Buddhist residential community in Birmingham, England, and has chosen to live with relatively little personal money. Dominic lives alone in an apartment in central London and is relatively wealthy.

Both of us teach, but right now we do that in rather different ways. Kulananda, the president of several centers of the Friends of the Western Buddhist Order, teaches primarily in that context, as well as through his writing. Dominic is an adjunct associate professor at the London Business School and also runs seminars and teaching programs for companies around the world.

Both of us have experience in the world of business. After taking his MBA at Stanford, Dominic worked as a management consultant with the Boston Consulting Group before becoming Director of Strategy at Blue Circle Industries in London, an international construction materials company. Kulananda founded

Windhorse Trading, an import-export firm that today employs 100 people in Cambridge, England, all of them practicing Buddhists. It has annual sales of $15 million, makes profits of $1.75 million and each year gives away about $850,000 to various Buddhist charities. None of the executives at Windhorse earns more than those working on the warehouse floor. As a rule, everyone has agreed to a salary that covers rent, food, utilities and other expenses, six weeks of retreats each year, plus fifty dollars of personal spending money each week. Kulananda lives more or less the same way. Dominic, who does freelance consulting for major corporations around the world, earns considerably more.

Both of us are ordained Buddhists, members of the Western Buddhist Order, and our first working partnership came about when we set out to launch an ethical banking initiative for the Friends of the Western Buddhist Order in conjunction with Triodos Bank, an ethical bank with a branch in the UK. Working together on that project, we became friends. We always knew we would collaborate again sometime, although we wouldn't have guessed it would be on this book.

In our different ways, we've both had to engage quite deeply with the world of money, and to make sense of the way we go about earning and spending. There have been times, for both of us, when that has been a struggle. Even in the course of writing this book, we've discovered aspects of our relationships to the world of money that we've needed to clarify or explore further. Working together on this project has been very fruitful for both of us and we hope the results will be equally helpful to the reader.

Buddhist centers in Europe and America attract a wide range of people, who earn and spend money in many different ways. As they try to integrate their money lives with their Buddhist practice, they face the kinds of issues that this book addresses. But very few of these people are really poor. Our typical reader, we imagine, will be rather like those who attend Buddhist classes in western cities, and very few live in extreme poverty. We have not forgotten, however, that most Buddhists in the world do not enjoy the relative affluence of their western counterparts. Our own Buddhist organization, for example, was founded in the West, but many of its members live in India, where they mostly come from communities that were formerly regarded as Untouchable under the Hindu caste system. These fellow Buddhists are among the poorest and most socially excluded members of an impoverished country. As we see our Indian Buddhist friends living effective spiritual lives in such difficult circumstances, we recognize how fortunate we are to face the problems of earning and spending that our book describes.

To write this book, we have drawn not only on our own experiences but also on those of many others. Some people who have helped us with teachings and stories are identified by name in these pages, others appear in a fictional guise. And there are many whose advice and teachings are not directly represented, though they have deeply informed our exploration of the subject.

Just like us, some people whom you'll meet in the book are well off, others have little that they can call their own. Whether rich or poor, they are all attempting to live a Buddhist life, and the examples taken from those lives have something to say to everyone, irrespective of wealth.

Within these pages, we've adopted a convention to distinguish characters whom we've invented purely for the purpose of illustration from those who actually exist. When you first encounter them in the text, we refer to real people either by a Buddhist name or by a first name and surname whether or not they've been slightly disguised for personal reasons. Those who have Western first names only are fictional. We've chosen to use Buddhist names when that is how the individuals are most often known in their working context. In many Buddhist traditions those who are ordained, whether living and working in the world or in the context of an established Buddhist institution, have been named to directly reflect their connection with Buddhism. Kulananda, for example, was given his name on ordination and uses it with his friends and family, as well as in his capacity as a Buddhist teacher. When he worked at Windhorse Trading, however, he was known to most of his suppliers and customers as Michael. Professor Houlder, on the other hand, remains Dominic in the broad context of his professional work and the friends, students and clients he has within it, but is Mahaprabha within the Buddhist community.

Who is this book for? Many who read it will have an interest in Buddhism. Some may already be Buddhist practitioners. Others may want to know what contemporary Buddhism has to do with the complex and often personally difficult realm of money. In today's Western society, earning and spending money inevitably consume a lot of our time and energy, no matter how worldly or spiritual we consider ourselves to be. Whether you're a committed Buddhist or fresh to its ideas and practices, we hope this book will help you to make more sense of your relationship to money matters.

Buddhism has always aimed to prevent people from splitting their lives between the material and spiritual worlds and instead to find ways to lead a whole life. It has a great deal to offer to help us to make our lives in relation to money whole. Some who read this book will have difficulties with money because they have far too little of it. Others, given the nature of our Western world, will have difficulties arising from having too much—certainly by the standards of most of the rest of the world. From whichever direction you approach the subject, we hope this book will help you to develop a healthy and balanced attitude to the question of earning and spending.

# Acknowledgments

This book draws extensively on the experience of Buddhists—practicing across a broad range of traditions—whom we interviewed in the United States and Great Britain. Sometimes we've quoted from these interviews, other times we haven't, but always they enriched our thinking and helped us to probe deeper into the subject. Our first thanks go to these generous people who were willing to share their lives with us: Norman Fischer, Ajahn Amaro, Bhikshuni Thubten Chodron, Kulamitra, Norma Coers, Viveka, Marc Lieberman, Karunadevi, Alan Senauke, Sudhana, Mel Ziegler, Betty Cook, Barr Rosenburg, Marc Lesser, Viradhamma, Les Kaye, Bill Scheinman, Colette Fanning, Dennis Schmidt, Fay Simpson, Vajraketu, Vijaya-mala, Ruchiraketu, Matthew Webb, Rosemary Tennison, Shantipala, Lokamdhara, Ed Piercy, Sahamati, Lokanatha, Vajrasamaya and Valerie Kenyon.

While visiting the States, Kulananda received kindness and hospitality above and beyond the call of duty from so many. Thank you,

Blossom, Vajramati, Karunadevi and Tony, Viveka, Collette and Su-
varnaprabha.

Reading and commenting incisively on a book in its evolving
stages, while simultaneously encouraging its authors is a task that
requires patience, rigor and kindness. Our special thanks go to
friends who undertook this task: Ruchiraketu, Achara, Achalavajra,
Jean-Paul Baillaud, John Campbell, Susanna Campbell, Lynda Grat-
ton and Gay Haskins.

Our agent, Susan Lee Cohen, of Riverside Literary Agency, has
been unfailingly supportive and enthusiastic about this project and
our editor at Broadway, Kris Puopolo, always knew what we were
driving at and helped to make it all clearer.

Behind the scenes there are those whose lives and work have
given us the inspiration to write on the subject of mindfulness and
money. These include our Buddhist teacher, Sangharakshita;
Michael Ray, who has opened many students' eyes to spirituality in
business at Stanford Business School; and the late Peter Wilcox,
shipowner, mentor and spiritual adventurer.

# Introduction

*No money, no spiritual life!*
*Money is humanity's greatest invention.*

Were you surprised to find grossly material statements at the start of a book on spirituality? You shouldn't be.

Money is an almost magical invention. Look in your wallet or purse right now and find the bits of paper. One of those scraps, perhaps an old shopping list, is good for little more than lighting a reluctant barbecue. But another, just as crumpled, with some worn green printing, lets you own the barbecue itself.

Today we use tatty pieces of green paper as money, or—even more mysterious—we use those little electronic bursts that somehow show up as numbers on a bank statement. Long ago, instead of greenbacks people used wampum (shells strung as beads) on the North American continent. They used cowry shells in ancient India, carried loose. Roman soldiers used salt. Prisoners favor cigarettes as money as they did in Germany after World War II. What do these currencies have in common? You can carry or otherwise transmit them, they won't perish quickly and one piece is very much like another. But the crucial common factor is that societies decided to believe that these things—perhaps of little or no worth in themselves—have value. That's an extraordinary, hugely beneficial act of the imagination, a shared illusion that underpins our civilized world.

No money: no civilization. What would life be like if you, with your family, had to do everything yourself? Grow your own food, build your own home and cut the timber for it too. Make your clothes and spin the yarn, write any book that you might read on paper of your own making. It might sound a little romantic and pure, even spiritual, but it wouldn't feel that way for long. Most of us would starve, soon. But even if you were one of the hardy ones who didn't starve, you'd spend every waking moment foraging, working, sweating, aching—all just to scratch out an existence.

That's how we learned, millennia ago, that we need each other, if only to win back time for the leisure to do more than survive. We began to divide up the tasks so that we could each do a few things well, and barter what we had, but didn't need, for something that someone else could provide. But that system had its limits. If I had extra bread, and you had some spare fuel, we could swap only if we were in exactly the same place and at exactly the same time. That way, we'd rarely have the chance to exchange what we'd grown or made beyond our little village and we'd miss out on so many opportunities to make life easier. "Wouldn't it be wonderful," someone must have asked, "if I could exchange things without having to find just the right person, right here and right now." And an entire culture wanted that so much that they agreed to hallucinate, to imagine that something intrinsically worthless—like a cowry shell (or a dollar bill)—could represent the fuel, or the bread or the computer software that some had and others needed, now or later.

This is money—a triumph of mind over the material world. It means that we can rise above barter: that we don't have to buy and sell at the same time, in the same place, with the same person. The manmade miracle of money can enhance life, stretching our imagination and opening up new, inspiring possibilities. Like many powerful instruments, money is a sharp, double-edged sword that can bring us complex wonders or much of the suffering that we know. But let's be clear. Whether it's used well or badly, money itself is the bedrock of everything that brings us freedom from the basic struggle to survive. No money, no civilization. No civilization, no spirituality. Few of us could be concerned with Enlightenment in a world of brutish enslavement to mere survival. There would be no time or energy available for it.

That's why it shouldn't be a surprise to find a Buddhist book celebrating money on the first page. As we have seen, money and its power are mind-made, called into being by our collective imagination.

Buddhism itself is about the mind and the way it creates the world we live in. The purpose of this book is to unleash the power of our own minds over money, to create a better world for us and for others.

## Money in Our World and in Our Minds

Today, thanks to money and what money makes possible, most of us live lives of luxury beyond the dreams of medieval princes. We may not live in castles, but our dwellings, if usually smaller, are far more comfortable, with air-conditioning and central heating, than ancient, princely habitats—and there are fewer marauding neighbors. We can fly to distant countries, drive hundreds of miles in a few hours, call friends in far-off places just to chat. We don't have to rub a magic lamp for exotic food and drink to appear: for many of us the take-out menu does the job. Entertainment at a finger's flick is limitless. The Internet puts more knowledge at our disposal than we could ever imagine exploring. Medical care provides the extra years in which we can enjoy it all. Education enriches our experience of the world and for those who can afford them, mutual funds and pension plans allow us to enjoy that experience with a degree of future security that would have astonished even our well-off forefathers, who contended with a much more precarious life. If you're feeling poor, think of what you already have that other generations could barely have imagined.

Over time, money has created an Aladdin's Cave of choice for us. It sometimes seems as if no aspect of human life is left untouched by it.

"Money brings honor, friends, conquests and realms," said John Milton, the great seventeenth-century English poet. Today, it can even buy youth, of sorts, if you'll take your chance with that cosmetic surgeon or jar of moisturizer. The song says you can't buy love, but candlelit dinners have been known to spark romance and dinners out don't always come easily if you're broke. "With money in your pocket," as the old Jewish proverb puts it, "you are wise and handsome, and you sing well too."

That's what money does for us. So how do we feel about its role in our lives?

Consider these statements:

- "Money? I really couldn't tell you how much I spent on what last year, or what I've got."
- "I love shopping. It makes me feel so good when other things aren't quite right. But sometimes I come back from the mall and I just can't remember why I bought all that stuff. Months later those clothes are still looking at me from the closet."
- "We're earning so much more than when we first moved in together. It was hard then to make ends meet, but we miss those days. We used to have fun hanging out with our friends, we got out to the country on the weekend. Now it's like an endless grind, just to keep our heads above water."
- "I'd love to do a job that's about me and what I care about, but let's get real. Dreams stay dreams when you've got college tuition, the mortgage and who knows what else to pay."
- "I get ill when I think about the way the market's dropped

since the bubble burst. I worked so hard to save a few thousand dollars. Where has it gone?"

▾ "I was just getting it together, and then I had to find a caregiver for my mom. It's cleaning me out. Who's going to do that for me when I get old?"

▾ "Look, if you're young like me, there's quite enough to think about just finding a job and paying the rent. Wise reflections on money and the meaning of work are for older people who already have a career."

If that first statement—about not knowing how much you have, or where it goes—hit home, then you're in good company. It's been said that many of us find it easier to tell a therapist about our sex lives than to talk about money with our accountants. We just don't want to know. And yet people in the United States work longer hours for more weeks a year than the inhabitants of any other industrialized country. A higher proportion of the population is employed and Americans spend more per head than anyone else on the planet. A person's relationship to money—earning and spending it—takes up more time and energy than any other activity: it's the biggest relationship that we have.

Think about your relationship with your life partner. If you are completely unaware that you *have* a relationship, it's unlikely to be a good one. The same holds for our relationship to money—whether we're rich, poor, or in between.

The rest of the statements are expressions of the suffering that's often found in relationship to money. Maybe you feel a little uneasy about your spending habits, or remember the good things that you no longer enjoy because the need to earn money leaves you insufficient time. Perhaps the way you earn leaves you unfulfilled, and the thought of an impoverished future hurts and paralyzes. This is suffering. It's not the acute, crippling pain of the really disadvantaged in the underclass or in the developing world, but it's the constant nagging sense that we're not crafting the marvelous lives that we might for ourselves, for others and the world. It's the kind of muted suffering that makes it hard for many ordinary people to rise to their true potential.

The Buddha's first teaching was about suffering, an experience that all humanity has in common:

> Birth is suffering, aging is suffering, sickness is suffering, death
> is suffering, sorrow and tears, pain, grief and despair are
> suffering, being bound up with what you hate is suffering,
> being parted from what you love is suffering, not to get what
> you want is suffering . . .[1]

Buddhism shows us ways to live that help us cut out the roots of pain and fear, so that we can really live.

## Money: What the Buddha Said

Turn the word "Buddhist" over in your mind. With your eyes closed, what do you see?

Many of us will conjure up a picture of a monk, the kind we are likely to meet in many parts of the East today: shaven headed, robed in orange. They might live in highly regulated, beautiful, well-endowed monasteries, but you won't see money and personal possessions. They're not allowed to have them. The early monks and nuns who followed the Buddha in India had even less. Like the Buddha, they were wanderers, homeless persons. Their robes were made of rags or shrouds from the cemetery. The orange dye was mud. They lived on whatever scraps of food the local villagers might give them, and they made a point of begging from the poor as well as from the better off. Although they lived as beggars, gifts of money

---

1. Vinaya Mahavagga Khandaka i.

were forbidden. Monks and nuns were not allowed even to touch it. And they still can't to this day in those traditions that have stayed unchanged since the Buddha was alive, over 2,500 years ago.

So here is one radical Buddhist solution to the pain and fear associated with spending and earning money: just don't do it. Don't have it. For these very tough men and women, the ideal way of life was and is to live contentedly "with robes sufficient to protect the body and alms food for the body's needs, taking just these, as a bird on the wing flies only with the load of its wings."[2]

However, this is by no means the sole Buddhist solution. In fact, only a tiny minority of Buddhists could ever become monks or nuns, entirely dependent on other people who were earning money to fill those begging bowls.

The Buddha had many disciples who were not living a monastic lifestyle. He had kings as followers, and the Buddha himself had been born into a powerful ruling family. Some of his disciples had made a lot of money through their work, like Anathapindika, who was the equivalent of an investment banker, or Ambapali, who was a famous royal courtesan.

Looking at the earliest records, the Buddha himself had a two-pronged approach to economic life. On the one hand there were the "homeless"—monks and nuns—who kept themselves rigorously apart from the world of money. On the other hand there were the laypeople—or "householders," as the Buddhist scriptures describe them—out there working, earning and spending. Laypeople supported the monks and nuns, but there was much more to it than that. Being a layperson was never meant merely to support a spiritual elite. Far from it: the Buddha's teachings were meant to transform anyone's life, regardless of lifestyle.

"Nothing in the world is worse than money," said Sophocles, one of ancient Greece's great thinkers. "It lays waste cities; it sets

---

2. Anguttara Nikaya II, 209.

men to roaming from home; it seduces and corrupts honest men and turns virtue to business; it teaches villainy and impiety." Many religious teachers and other philosophers might agree with Sophocles, but not the Buddha. For the Buddha never condemned wealth in itself. He might have warmed to the compassionate idealism of the Haight-Ashbury flower children or the early Israeli kibbutzniks, but as a supreme realist, he would have known that getting rid of money doesn't work for very long, and that those communities couldn't last. The Buddha looked unswervingly at what the world presented to him and judged what lay behind it with complete objectivity. He would have known that the Utopian attempts to do away with wealth in our own era on a larger scale could only make humanity's best achievements come crashing down in ruins. From a Buddhist standpoint, the grim misery of life in the old socialist economies of Eastern Europe and Russia, or horrific experiments like Pol Pot's attempt to abolish money in Cambodia, stem from an appalling lack of objective intelligence. Get rid of money, and you undo the whole complex chain of human interdependence.

In fact the Buddha had a lot to say in praise of wealth and money. The issues for him concerned how you get it and what you do with it: whether you are using its energy to make yourself happier, or to make the world better.

One of his earliest and richest disciples, King Pasenadi, told the Buddha that he was winding up the affairs of a recently deceased miser who had lived in the kingdom. Auditors had found eighty million gold coins and a lot of silver, all of which was being shipped to Pasenadi's palace because the miser had died without making a will. Had he forgotten? Our guess is that there was nobody he cared about, no cause that he was interested in enough to leave it to. So Pasenadi got it all, like some ancient version of the IRS. And this miser had lived a miserable life, despite all his wealth. The scriptures say that his diet was a sour gruel of rice husks left over from the day before. He could have traveled in style, but instead he went around in a small, decrepit cart with a flimsy awning made of leaves.

The Buddha was far from impressed by this impoverished lifestyle. Here was an example of someone with tremendous wealth who made nothing of it. As a miser, of course he didn't give his money to the monks and nuns, but the sad waste went further than that. "A miser doesn't use it to please himself, his parents, his wife and children, nor his slaves, craftsmen and servants, his friends and colleagues," said the Buddha. "His wealth, not being rightly used, is either confiscated by kings, taken by robbers, burnt by fire or swept away by flood. Or it is taken by heirs for whom he has no affection. His riches, not being rightly used, run to waste, not to enjoyment." Using one of the beautiful images that we so often find in the scriptures when the Buddha speaks, he continues: "It is like a lake of crystal clear, cool, delicious water. Beautiful, surrounded by good shores, but lying in a savage region. No one can drink from it or bathe in it, or make any use of it at all. Such are the riches of a miser."

But if a generous man acquires great wealth, the Buddha said: "His case is like that of the beautiful lake I spoke of, but now it lies near a village or town where people can draw water and drink from it, bathe in it and use it for any other purpose. His riches go to enjoyment, not to waste."[3]

The Buddha told his banker disciple Anathapindika that wealth—well used—should first and foremost give pleasure to us and our families. Then there's the pleasure that we can give to our friends and others who live around us. And there's more—having wealth means that we can recover when things go wrong for us. Wealth means that we can keep up a good reputation in the community (by making ritual offerings in the Buddha's day, which were no doubt costly) and it means that we can enable the good causes

---

3. Samyutta Nikaya i, 88.

that we find most worthwhile (traditionally that meant gifts to monks and nuns).⁴ The crucial point is that we make full use of our wealth: to engage happily with others and with the world. The same goes for the way we earn our money:

> *The wise and virtuous shine forth like beacons.*
> *Those who acquire their wealth in harmless ways*
> *Like bees that honey gather—*
> *Riches mount up for them*
> *Like ant-hills' rapid growth.⁵*

So true Buddhist economics is not about building Utopia where wealth and money have been abolished. Nor do you have to become a monk or nun, although, as you'll see, there is a lot to learn from these as well as other traditional Buddhist ways of life. But to be of help to us, traditional Buddhist teaching about money needs to be reinterpreted in today's Western context.

### Bringing the Buddha's Teaching to the West

Buddhism developed in a feudal world of peasants, clans and kings. Although there were merchants, bankers and craftsmen living in small towns, this was a rural society. Few people could read. It was a much simpler existence than ours. But then, from its origin in Northern India, Buddhism moved around the globe, spreading south into Sri Lanka, north into Tibet and the Himalayan region, and east into China, Japan, Korea and South East Asia. As it did so, it constantly encountered new conditions, and new variants of Buddhism began to flourish. Today, half the world's population live

---

4. Anguttara Nikaya V. 41, Adiya Sutta.
5. Digha Nikaya 31, iii, 188, Sigalaka Sutta.

in countries that are, or have been, influenced by the Buddha's teachings.

Buddhist teachings have only very recently started to be applied seriously in the West. As the teachings arrive here, they are encountering a set of conditions that are radically different from anything that they have ever encountered before. If we want to understand what Buddhism has to say about money in our lives today, we need to work it out from what the Buddha himself said about the subject in very different circumstances. To do so, we must go to the heart of his teachings and to the heart of what the various traditional forms of Buddhism have had to say about money, and then re-express it in Western terms for a Western context.

Here are some of the crucial differences in interpreting Buddhist teachings on money.

First of all, when Buddhism meets the West it is coming up against a more highly developed culture than any—perhaps apart from China—that it has ever come upon before. When Buddhist missionaries entered other societies in the East for the first time, they generally brought a higher culture with them. Sometimes Buddhism brought literacy. The Tibetans, for example, had no written language before they became Buddhists. But Western culture is highly developed, powerful and confident. And it has a well-developed language for discussing money, alongside which traditional Buddhist discourse can seem naive. In the West we must listen particularly attentively and imaginatively if we are to hear the Buddha's teachings about money.

The second crucial difference is that in the West most of us have many more choices than people had in traditional Buddhist countries. There, ordinary individuals remained in the state to which they were born and were not free to challenge it. They didn't have democratic voting rights or spending power. And their lives were structured around a fairly rigid set of clan and extended family relationships, which have largely broken down in the West. The extraordinary breadth of choice that we face—of family structure and lifestyles, ways to earn and ways to spend—can feel like liberation or unparalleled confusion. Buddhism has a tougher challenge guiding us through those choices than it faced in the Eastern world.

The third difference is that the way we earn and spend money in the West has the potential to do more harm—or good—than ever before. Increasingly, money matters, far more than in the Buddha's time. Forests are disappearing, species are dying out, pollution is widespread, global inequalities produce widespread suffering, resources are consumed and not replaced and climate change is happening at a frightening rate. There is a great deal that Buddhism could say about all of this, but it has never been called upon previously to address these issues.

It is true that all of these factors—cultural development, freedom and environmental crisis—are currently found in many of the Asian countries where Buddhism still thrives, but the patterns of Buddhist practice that continue to be found in those countries were first laid down under very different circumstances. Only in the West today is Buddhism encountering the modern world afresh. Buddhism has a great deal to offer the modern world, but it has to learn to speak its ancient wisdom with a new voice, so that its old and time-honored disciplines and practices can find fresh channels of expression.

Perhaps most important, as Buddhism emerges in the West, the former divide between monks, nuns and laypeople, which played such a large part in Buddhist history in the East and governed relationships to money, is far less significant. Large numbers of those Westerners who have fully committed themselves to Buddhist practice do not follow a monastic lifestyle. Previously, in the East, you were either a productive, and reproductive, member of society or you became a monk or nun. There was little space in between these two options. But since the 1960s in the West, with the decline of our traditional, largely Christian ways of characterizing social relationships, with the advent of birth control, and with hugely increased social and physical mobility, that space has opened wide. The challenge for Buddhism is to explore and chart that new space. Western Buddhists are eagerly experimenting with new ways of living, working and consuming. This book gives you the chance to join them, to engage in your own bold experiment with money.

## Money, Self and Suffering

Have you ever felt that there is something, just out of reach, that will make your life complete if only you had it? That sense that there's something vast but indefinable missing in our lives is an essential part of the basic human experience. Sometimes that hole is scarily yawning open before us. Sometimes we're half-aware of it.

We'll do everything we can to fill that void. For thousands of years, misuse of alcohol and other drugs from opiates to cigarettes have featured as solutions. Most of us have hoped that a loved one, or a vocation, will fill that hole and give us—in the literal sense— fulfillment. Sometimes we avoid that sense of incompleteness by keeping busy. There's nothing like a hectic family life, or a demanding job, to take the edge off incompleteness. And of course there's money. Money provides the power to reach out and make almost anything ours. It's so easy for us to promise ourselves that this will make our lives complete. But it doesn't.

At this point Buddhism has something to say that isn't easy. It's a message that strikes right at the heart of the problem of incompleteness:

*Money will not make your life complete. In fact, nothing will.*

Nothing whatsoever will make your life complete: not possessions, not a job, not a family, not a vocation, or a loved one, nor drugs, nor religion, not even Buddhism. That's because of the way life is, and suffering comes from our determined attempts to swim against the flow of life.

Why do we do this? More than anything else, the Buddha said, we want to *be*. Craving of that kind, he said, is the root of our suffering:

> This is the Noble Truth of the Origin of Suffering: it is . . .
> craving for the fulfillment of our obsessive desires, craving for
> being, craving for non-being.[6]

When we crave to be, we want our very own lives to have paramount importance, to live at the very center of the universe with the world revolving around us, affirming our own existence. In our darkest moments, when we might wish that we'd never been born, we mirror the same conceit: we desire non-being, to get rid of the whole universe.

The idea that we can fulfill such craving is a fantasy, a complex of delusions, which the Buddha's teaching sets out to strip away. Many contemporary adherents of the later development of Buddhism known as the Mahayana cherish a short scripture called the Heart Sutra. In its opening verses, Avalokitesvara, an archetypal Buddhist figure who represents the principle of limitless compassion, looks down on the world and its suffering. In several traditional explanations of the Sutra, we are told that Avalokitesvara first of all sees us caught in everyday pain and frustration. Then he sees the sadness of our dying. But he also sees us, saddest of all, as laboring under the delusion of our cosmic self-importance. And, as the Sutra tells us, if anyone can overcome that great delusion then,

> . . . *Holding to nothing whatever,*
> *But dwelling in the perfection of wisdom*
> *He is free from delusive hindrance*
> *Rid of the fear bred by it*
> *And in the end he attains to Nirvana.*

6. Vinaya Mahavagga Khandaka i.

All of the many schools of Buddhist teaching echo the Heart Sutra by teaching that we have to come to grips with the misleading illusion about the primacy of the self if we want to live life at its best. They say that there are three dimensions to our problematic sense of self-importance. We will take each in turn.

The first is the illusion that we have a *permanent* self.

Intellectually, it is not hard to see that everything—ourselves included—is in a constant state of flux. Everyone changes a lot over a lifetime, and we all die eventually. Our "self," then, is a temporary pattern that holds together for an alarmingly short time. But a temporary pattern isn't a very flattering or appealing state for most of us. So, even if we can appreciate the idea of impermanence, we'll often behave as if it wasn't so. We'll do our best to prevent change with anything at our disposal. We'll use money to pile up possessions around us to get a sense of permanence and security, like Egyptian pharaohs who hoped to find immortality by building pyramids.

Think of the ways in which we earn and spend money to reinforce our sense of security. It might be the job that leaves us frustrated each evening but that we can't bring ourselves to leave, because we can't imagine a different future and we fear the unknown. It might be unwise speculation on the equity markets in the hope that our winnings will leave us financially secure for as long as we live. We might know people who scrape and save to make the payments on that large dream home, making of it a permanent symbol of having made something of their lives. But then they might find that their wants become very different as retirement approaches, and that the dream home has become an unexpected burden. They might have missed out on opportunities to do much more imaginative and satisfying things with their money as their needs—if they only saw them clearly—kept changing along the way. If we cling to the idea of permanence, we'll find it harder to cope with life's unexpected turnings, good or ill.

The second dimension of our self-centered delusion is that we have a *separate* self.

This is our sense of needing to act on our sense of incompleteness on our own terms, regardless of what's going on for everyone else. But the reality is that our lives are interwoven with the lives of others, and if we try to live without considering the fundamentally shared nature of existence then the attempt will end in tears. We'll try to deal with our sense of incompleteness by taking this new lover, that new digital camera, creating a perfect little world inside our personal gated community, burning up a lot of money as we do so. The return on this investment will be very disappointing: in fact it will be less than zero. That's because the more we make things ours, as opposed to anyone else's, the more we reinforce the painful sense of separateness from other human beings and the world. It's the very sense of being separate that leaves us feeling incomplete.

And finally, traditional Buddhist schools say that we need to banish the notion of a *substantial* self.

We meet someone new and they want to know who we are. "Tell me about yourself," they say. And usually, we have a well-crafted story, a story that neatly packages who we are as a concise personal introduction. The short version might highlight the job or the family. With a longer telling, the story of who we are will develop and get richer, but it will remain a partial story that we tell ourselves as well as others, a story that fixes our identity. Money will be very close to the surface of the story, shaping a great deal of our identity, because we do a lot of earning and spending. The clothes we wear, the address we live at, the car we drive, what we read and eat: all these help to give a sense of who we are to others and ourselves. But there's far more to us than this. We have to tell our stories selectively and there's a lot that we are bound to leave out.

The reality is that there are no limits to what we are: there's an endless flux of changing processes that can't be contained by a particular identity. Clinging to a particular identity makes us miss out on so much of life that we're left feeling incomplete. And the more we try to shore up that narrow sense of who we are, the wider that hole of incompleteness gapes.

These views go to the heart of human suffering. We try to compensate for the sense of incompleteness by keeping up the pretence that we can *be*: as permanent, separate and substantial selves. We use our energy—including our money—to do so. When that delusion comes under threat, we might get anxious and tend to react with craving, greedily grasping whatever or whomever will shore up our sense of self. Or we might react with aversion. Aversion drives us to exclude or eliminate the things or people that threaten our sense of self: it's the force of hatred, be it muted or in full spate. But the more we grasp, the more we try to destroy, the more incomplete we feel.

That's a pretty miserable description of human life: a life in which we throw ourselves reactively from threatening event to threatening event as the deluded slave of our own greed and hatred. The good news is that life isn't always like that, and we can learn to live in a way that changes the picture radically; that helps us to become less deluded and reactive and instead, much wiser and more creative in our ability to master greed and hatred. Money, as raw energy, can fuel our reactive behavior. But it can also fuel a journey—the path of abundance—that any of us can choose to make toward an extraordinary creative life. It's up to us.

## The Path of Abundance: Getting Started

Let's try to imagine what life would be like if we were able to change our view of self, other and the world. What would it be like if we didn't have to be afraid of impermanence: if we could embrace life's surprises and use our money to break our stale routines? What would life be like if we used our money to break down the dividing walls that keep us separate from others, earning and spending it in ways that open up the joy of sharing our existence? And how would it be if we believed that we don't have to be trapped by a tight-packed, substantial identity: that there is always more to discover about who we are, that money can allow us to adventure into an uncharted realm in which anything is possible? What would it be like to make our lives less impoverished and more abundant?

Buddhist literature is full of descriptions of how the world might be for us if we could only relax that hard, closed-in, tight-packed sense of self and end the struggle against incompleteness. There's a famous image of the universe as a limitless web of magical jewels. They sparkle in every direction, "glittering like stars." Pick one of those jewels and look into its glowing core, the scriptures tell us, and you'll see that in its polished surface there are reflected all the other jewels in the web, infinite in number. Not only that, but each of the jewels reflected in this one jewel is also reflecting all the other jewels.[7] We might take each of those jewels as a life, sparkling with possibilities and glowing with the treasure of every other life at its core. But if we use our energy—our money—to unpick that extraordinary interwoven web of lives, then we will be truly poor. Those jewels don't exist unless they are reflected in each other.

To avoid that total impoverishment and to live abundantly, the challenge is to reverse our reactive, deluded response to our sense of incompleteness, and use our money to help us do so.

Scriptures from Mahayana Buddhism (the form that exists today in China, Japan, Korea, Vietnam and Tibet) hold up the ideal of the Bodhisattva, a highly advanced spiritual practitioner who lives

---

7. See Francis H. Cook, *Hua-yen Buddhism: The Jewel Net of Indra* (University Park: Pennsylvania State University Press, 1977).

his or her life entirely for the sake of others. These scriptures include the legend of Vimalakirti, an extremely wealthy Bodhisattva.

His wealth was inexhaustible but he used it chiefly to sustain the poor and the helpless. In fact, whatever he did, he did for others. He observed a pure morality in order to protect the immoral. To reconcile beings who were angry and violent, he maintained tolerance and self-control. He blazed with energy in order to inspire the lazy, maintained concentration and meditation in order to support the mentally troubled and achieved incisive wisdom in order to assist the foolish. He showed up at the sports fields and the casinos, but his aim was always to help develop those who were mindlessly attached to sports and gambling. He mixed in all crowds, yet was respected as foremost of all.

He engaged in all sorts of businesses, yet had no interest in profit or possessions. He would appear at crossroads and on street corners to teach people, and to protect them he participated in government. To help children develop, he visited all the schools. To demonstrate the evils of desire, he entered the brothels. He was honored as a businessman among businessmen because he was dedicated only to the truth and as a landlord among landlords because he renounced any aggression connected with ownership.[8]

Vimalakirti's name means "Stainless Repute": he could function in the world without being in any way tarnished.

Here is someone who had clearly gone all the way. Craving and aversion were left far behind as this Bodhisattva plunged creatively and exuberantly into life with his hefty bank balance. This may sound more than a little daunting for any of us struggling right here and now with our reactivity. Fortunately, we all have within us the sparks of a creative awareness. Quite naturally, we incline from time to time to feelings of generosity that connect us deeply with others: by no means is craving the whole story. We all have the ca-

---

8. See Robert Thurman, *The Holy Teaching of Vimalakirti* (University Park and London: Pennsylvania State University Press, 1983).

pacity to engage and love, as well as to recoil from life with aversion.

We can all consciously choose to develop those creative qualities, and there are a number of proven, practical methods for doing so. If we undertake that task, then we will begin to change our attitudes to money so that it becomes a means of bringing about positive change in ourselves and in the world around us, instead of it being a source of suffering. Money itself is neutral. We can use it as a means to reinforce an impoverished sense of who we are or as a means for going beyond it toward abundance. It is up to us.

If we decide to use our money to change our mind, to change craving into generosity, aversion into love and delusion into clear awareness, then our lives will become incomparably richer. We may or may not have more money as a result, but we will learn to use money and not be used by it.

The transformation of our deeply held attitudes to money calls for patience, dedication and understanding. But few tasks are more worthwhile.

Sometimes this will be hard going. But it should also be pleasurable. The Buddha had a very practical approach to teaching, and knew that almost all of us, as pleasure seekers, are unlikely to persevere with change—however worthwhile it might be—unless we find at least some pleasure along the way. This book distills the pleasure (as well as the hard work) that those we've met have found as they have taken charge of money in their lives. The many exercises and practices that we've been lent by the Buddhist tradition and contemporary teachers will enable you to get a lot more enjoyment from the way you spend, and bring more wisdom to it. You'll have the chance to build your confidence by becoming more and more imaginative in what you do with your money. You'll start to discover and enlarge your hidden wealth: using money to expand the ways you relate to others and the world. Over time, you'll gain the strength to make the way you earn your money more and more an expression of who you are. You'll make better decisions about your financial future as you lessen your anxiety about it. We want money to cost you less of your life, and to give you the room to live.

This may sound far removed from where we are today, and no transformation happens just from wishing it so. We'll need a strategy to make it happen. A good strategy sheds a clear, objective light on who we are now. It tells us how we arrived at where we are, and helps us to create a powerful, inspiring picture of what we hope to be, marking out the steps we need to take to get there. And it needs to do more. Few of us can claim that, right now, we know exactly what or who we want to be, far in the future. Today, that picture can only be provisional. So our strategy needs to help us learn. As we step toward our provisional goal, the path that we choose to go about the journey must help us to discover more about the destination, about what we most desire.

In those terms, the Buddha was the pre-eminent strategist. His very first teaching—known across the Buddhist world as the Four Noble Truths—is a strategist's account of suffering, looking at its reality, its origins, its ending and the way to end it. We are going to apply the same strategist's approach to our relationship with money. We'll better understand our money lives and the forces compelling us to earn and spend in unmindful ways that cause suffering and limit our potential for happiness, that impoverish and deny possibilities for abundance. We'll create a path to explore specific ways to bring about change, and assess what a range of committed Buddhist practitioners have accomplished in crafting a creative relationship with money. You'll start to uncover your own destination: becoming more aware of your purpose in getting money and spending it.

Along the way, you'll find that money, like any source of energy, can be a means to help you move forward on the Path of Abundance. C. S. Lewis's Narnia stories are still popular with many children and adults too. In his *Silver Chair,* we meet the cheerful gnomes from the land of Bism deep below the Earth's crust, who mined living jewels beside rivers of fiery gold in which the salamanders swam. You could pick bunches of diamonds and drink the juice of blazing rubies. The air underground was rich, hot, spicy and made you sneeze. There was no comparison to be made with the cold, dead gemstones that lay closer to the surface. Here we'll be mining deep, to find the kind of money that can set lives aglow and transform ourselves and the world.

# PART ONE

## The Wheel of Money

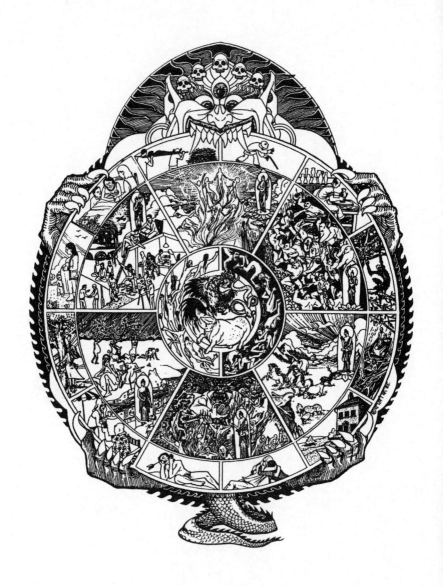

# ONE

٧ ٧ ٧ ٧ ٧ ٧ ٧

# The Six Worlds: Creating the Realms That Confine Us

If you go to any part of the Himalayan Buddhist world and visit the many temples and shrine rooms, you'll see some rather fearsome images. In one image, a huge fire-breathing monster holds up a great wheel in its claws. The monster is called *yama-raja,* the "Lord of Impermanence," and the wheel he holds up has come to be known in the West as the Wheel of Life.

The Wheel of Life is one of the most ancient, widespread and highly developed images in all of Buddhism. It tells us who we are and how things came to be as they are. It is a mirror to look into, and what we see reflected in it is none other than ourselves.

Like all great symbols, the Wheel can be interpreted in any number of ways and can be used for a wide variety of purposes. In the next few chapters we will use it to examine more deeply how our attitudes to money shape us and our world from moment to moment.

The Wheel is divided into four concentric circles. Each of these describes a particular aspect of the complex process by which we become what we are in any given moment.

The Wheel of Life can be used to shed light on any aspect of human behavior. Looked at from the mainly economic perspective it takes on a particular character. It becomes what we will call the Wheel of Money.

Let's look at each of the four circles in turn and see what they have to tell us about the world of money and how our attitudes to it form and re-form us from moment to moment.

## The Six Worlds

The largest of the four circles that make up the Wheel is the third from the center. Further divided into six segments, each of these parts of the circle depicts a different world.

The topmost world is that of the gods. In this segment we see the gods at ease in their palaces, listening to music, drinking in the beauty all around them. Next comes the world of the jealous-gods. The sworn enemies of the gods, these fierce warriors live only for battle and trust no one. Then comes the world of the animals, where we see different beasts browsing, hunting or lying in the sun, doing what animals do. The bottommost world is a hell, where demons inflict all kinds of tortures and miseries on the anguished inhabitants. After that we see the hungry ghosts' world, a gray desolate realm peopled by beings in states of acute unsatisfiable desire. Finally we reach the human world, where we see all kinds of men and women going about their lives, working, studying, resting and playing.

This does not mean that only one of the six worlds need concern us humans. Far from it. We all experience all of these different worlds in the course of our money lives, sometimes in a single afternoon. To demonstrate, we introduce Maria, a computer programmer. Let's examine some of the different states of mind, different worlds even, that she passes through in that short space of time.

We meet her at the entrance to her apartment, a small backpack on her back and a tote bag in one hand. She's been working out at her gym and has just arrived home, feeling really satisfied. It's so good to exercise after a day's work; it makes her feel human again. After eight hours in front of her computer screen she can feel so numb. Her boyfriend's away on a business trip and if she's not careful she'll just spend her evenings blobbed-out in front of the television with pizza and a beer. Closing the apartment door behind her, she pulls a new pair of shoes from the tote bag and stares ruefully at them. That's her third new pair this month! What is it with her? She was determined to pass that new shoe store and go straight to the gym, but she'd glanced in the window, one little look, and there they were, so right for this spring, just begging to be bought. They looked so cute, and they'd be perfect with those new linen pants . . . Perfect? Now that she's home, they don't seem all that different from the first pair she bought this month, and she wasn't sure about the heel on those either . . . Why does she keep doing this, she asks herself, how many pairs of shoes does a girl really need? With a twinge of guilt, she thinks momentarily of the homeless man she saw sitting outside the store. What could he have done with the ninety-five dollars those shoes cost?

Mildly disgusted with herself, she stuffs her gym clothes into the washing machine, flops into her work chair and clicks on e-mail. For the past six months she's been working from home, programming for a major software company. The pay is good and at first she could set her own hours, which let her continue with her artwork as well as taking the odd coffee break with one of her many friends. But she misses the daily companionship of an office, and lately Tony, her team leader, has been pushing the team for more hours. The firm just lost a major client and budgets are being squeezed. Maria wants more compensation for the time she's putting in and she's e-mailed Tony to that effect.

She has mail. It's from work, and written in Tony's customary blunt style. There's no chance of a raise, don't even think about it. In fact, considering the pressure they're under right now, they should all stand by to contribute that little bit more.

Maria hits the roof. That jerk! He doesn't know what it's like living her life. And he doesn't care anyway. How can he ask for more? She hasn't painted in months. The twinges in her wrist may be the onset of carpal tunnel. She hardly sees another living person all day. . . .

She stomps about the apartment and kicks a few chairs. No, she's not having this anymore. No way. She's quitting. In fact, she's more than quitting. She's going to start a website for exploited people like herself. She'll show that dumb firm you can't treat people like this. Just wait till people read about their working practices. Tele-commuting? It's more like a sweatshop in your own apartment! There will be plenty of people with horror stories to tell, all she has to do is get networking!

Maria can't bear to be in the same room as her computer any longer. She storms out of the apartment, slamming the door, and pounds down the stairs and onto the sidewalk. Head down, shoulders hunched, she heads for the park. On the third steaming circuit of the lake something suddenly catches her attention. A clump of anemones sparkle in the sunlight. Yellow against green—the tones are just perfect. Maria stops in her tracks and stares. What an incredible spring light there is this afternoon. How could she have missed it? She raises her head. In a cobalt blue sky a single white seagull glides in circles above the lake. She feels the tension drain from her body as she leans on the railings, taking in the scene, feeling the breeze on her cheek, all thoughts of work evaporated.

She stands there for half an hour, strangely content, her mind still and clear—bright with the beauty all around her. Then suddenly, from nowhere, she knows just what she'll do. She'll quit all right, and start a website. But forget the revenge, what a waste. No, she's going to sell artists' materials on the Web. She knows there's a market out there, she'd use it herself. So would some of her artist friends, friends she hasn't seen in ages. Wouldn't some of them love to be involved! Yes—it comes to her in a flash, just how to structure the site . . . She can't wait to call her friends and tell them.

▾ ▾ ▾

In the course of a not typical afternoon, we can see that Maria experienced a range of emotions and states of mind. If we look again, we'll see that she touched on each of the six worlds of the Wheel of Money in this short time.

Let's now look at each of these in turn.

## The Animal World

At the end of her day's work, Maria was not feeling truly human. She was in an animal state of mind and if she hadn't taken herself off to the gym to clear her head she might have passed yet another evening blobbed-out in front of the television with a take-out pizza. In the symbolism of the Wheel, animals don't have much regard for anything beyond food, sex and sleep and so long as these needs are met, they are not bothered with much else. When we're in an animal state of mind, we can't think creatively. We live—and work— just to exist.

Maria had the self-awareness to know that at the end of eight hours staring at the computer, an hour at the gym would restore her to a human state.

We're in an animal state of mind with regard to money when:

▾ We're stuck in the same rut, doing a job that means little to
  us, spending eight hours a day, forty-eight weeks a year,
  watching the clock and killing time.
▾ We spend each Saturday afternoon walking down the same
  supermarket aisles, putting the same items in our baskets as we

did last week and the week before and the week before, irrespective of price or quality, regardless of what goes into them and what effect they have on us or our environment.

▾ So long as we meet our bills, with a little over, we're happy. Because what else can you expect from life?

TRY THIS:

Do you ever get into an animal state of mind? What's that like for you? Describe what you do in the periods of your own animal existence. What causes you to enter the animal world? What causes you to leave it? Is it really as refreshing as it sometimes seems?

## The Hungry Ghosts

As soon as she looked into the window of her favorite shoe store, Maria was impelled to buy yet another pair of shoes, even though they weren't quite right for her and she'd bought a similar pair just a few weeks before. She'd fallen into the world of the hungry ghosts.

The hungry ghosts are driven by intense neurotic craving. Neurotic, because the craving they experience is often the displaced desire for something else—something they are not consciously aware of. Wanting affection, not knowing how best to go about getting it, they crave chocolate instead. Perhaps that was what their mothers always gave them when she wanted to express her affection. But no amount of chocolate, however good it is, can meet our real need for affection and so that craving is never satisfied. The shoes she bought clearly meant something to Maria, but they stand for something else, something she's not aware of. No matter how many pairs she buys she'll never be quite satisfied.

Hungry ghosts are traditionally depicted as gray, emaciated beings with gross, sagging bellies and long, constricted necks. They have huge, staring eyes; tiny, pinprick mouths; and their overall experience is one of unfulfilled longing. Whatever food they manage to get into their mouths right away turns to excrement, ash or fire. Aching with thirst, when they approach the water that flows through their world it recedes from them. The meager fruit that grows on the spindly trees is almost always out of reach, and when they do manage to pluck and eat one it turns to swords and daggers in their bellies. Hungry ghosts can never get enough.

We ourselves become hungry ghosts when:

- ▾ We buy things, not because we need them, or because we'll need them later and the price is reduced, but just because we want to buy *something,* anything almost.
- ▾ We try to control our spending but splurge on luxuries almost against our own wishes.
- ▾ We're suddenly obsessed with having a new bathroom, or a new car (even though our current one is still running fine), or another dinner service, or an obscure kitchen gadget we saw advertised once, and we can't rest and can't think of anything else until we get it.
- ▾ We become preoccupied with our savings, checking the balance every week, not giving or spending more than we absolutely have to, piling up money purely for its own sake.

TRY THIS:

Can you recognize any of the above states in your own experience? In what other ways might you be a hungry ghost?

What happens to you in the hungry ghost world? What causes you to enter that world and what causes you to leave it? Has getting what you wanted in that state ever really made your life better?

## The Hell Worlds

At all costs Maria tries to avoid engaging with the hell worlds. They're just too painful. She doesn't like to think too much about how the disheveled man sitting on the sidewalk outside the shoe store passes his nights, and what it must be like to live like that for nights on end, winter and summer. Whenever she starts to engage empathetically with the circumstances of homeless people, her mind just swerves away from the pain of it and she starts to think of something else. But even though she doesn't like to think about it, people like him are one of the reasons she keeps on working as she has. You must pay the rent!

Buddhism recognizes a number of different hell worlds whose occupants experience continuous torture and all kinds of deprivation, but none of these worlds lasts forever. There is no Buddhist equivalent of the idea of eternal damnation. But even though one may not live in a hellish state forever, the hells are terrible places to be.

Many people today find that the levels of stress associated with their work can produce quite hellish mental states. The stress builds up and up and they can't get rid of it. They come home feeling wired and leave for work the next morning all hyped up.

In the context of our money lives, we ourselves touch on the hell worlds when:

- ▾ We're trapped in painful jobs that we'd do anything to escape.
- ▾ We're bullied and harassed at work but can't quit.
- ▾ Our work generates intense levels of anxiety and tension that we cannot dispel.
- ▾ We're driven to keep going in our work purely out of fear of poverty.

TRY THIS:

Consider—have you ever experienced a hell realm? What causes you to enter a hell world and what causes you to leave it?

What would have helped you when you were in that state? Can you now do something for others who are in similar states?

## The Jealous-Gods

When Maria decided she would take revenge on her employers for what she thought of as their exploitation of her and her co-workers she found herself in the world of the jealous-gods.

The jealous-gods are aggressive people, highly driven, devoted to the conquest of enemies and the pursuit of wealth, fame and power. We find them in the worlds of business, the media, sports, the military and even in religious organizations. For many of them money earned is a marker of worth, telling the world just how good they are. The jealous-gods always want to be the best and they let no one get in their way.

According to Buddhist legend, the jealous-gods are constantly engaged in a warlike struggle with the gods for the possession of the wish-fulfilling tree. This tree has it roots in the jealous-gods' world but it grows up into the world of the gods where it bears its fruit. The gods reach over and pluck from this tree whatever they want. The jealous-gods want that fruit as well, but they are too busily engaged in their competitive activities to ever actually reach it. They have no time for leisure, no time for enjoyment. Enraged, they attack the tree and try to hack it down—hoping to get hold of the fruit that way.

The roots of the wish-fulfilling tree are in the jealous-gods' world. Many of the goods and services we enjoy these days were produced by them. But they themselves never really enjoy the fruits of their own labors. They always want more and can never rest with what they have achieved. There is always a new market to conquer, a new deal to be done, a better part to play, a competitor to beat, an enemy to humiliate.

We ourselves fall into the jealous-gods' world when:

- ▾ We deviously maneuver for promotion at work at the expense of our co-workers.
- ▾ We lie to advance our own cause or that of our firm.
- ▾ We use anger and our ability to inspire fear to get what we want, especially from those beneath us in the hierarchy at work.
- ▾ We want something because we hate the idea of someone else having what we don't.
- ▾ We use our sexuality to manipulate others at work.
- ▾ We are preoccupied with our relative status.
- ▾ We buy things for the sake of demonstrating our status and power.

TRY THIS:

Reflect—have you ever been a jealous-god? Did you ever get what you most deeply hoped for when you were in that state?

What happens when you dwell in the world of the jealous-gods? What causes you to enter this world and what causes you to leave it?

## The World of the Gods

After she caught sight of the clump of yellow anemones, Maria was suddenly projected into the world of the gods. This is a world of refinement, beauty and leisure; of artists, poets, musicians and meditators. According to Buddhist teaching, one of the difficulties people can have in the god world is that although it is a world of refined enjoyment, the gods tend not to do very much; their enjoyment tends to be rather passive. If they're not careful, when the factors that gave rise to their godlike state cease, they fall out of the god world and, bruised and bewildered by the relatively coarse worlds they then encounter, they fall into hell-like states, anguished by their loss. The god worlds have their place, but we can't depend on our access to them. For the very large majority of us, they are somewhere to visit, not somewhere to live.

There are, however, those who, because they have inherited wealth or earned a great deal of it, can devote themselves to lives of refinement and pleasure. Is there any ground for thinking that they shouldn't?

There are reasons why one might not feel easy about living in a god world—some good, some bad. Many of us living in the West today have feelings of irrational guilt tied up with our relationship to money. This comes from our Judeo-Christian heritage, and especially the Protestant work ethic that informs the cultures of Northern Europe and North America. Often we feel that we have somehow to "deserve" our wealth and unconsciously we may not feel at all worthy of having it.

From a Buddhist perspective, inherited wealth is often thought of as a consequence of good deeds done in past lives. But whether you're at ease with the idea of rebirth or not, inherited wealth is certainly nothing to be ashamed of or to feel guilty about. The relevant question is what happens next. You can use your wealth and the leisure it affords to cultivate your mind and to help others, or you can use it purely for self-indulgence. What you do with it now will determine what happens to you next.

If you look at the faces of people who've led mainly self-indulgent lives, they're often quite ugly and they're generally not at all at ease with themselves or others. The god worlds are all impermanent. They are pleasant enough for a time, but when circumstances change, as change they must, the former inhabitants of the god worlds, if they haven't used their opportunities well, are left in a pretty sorry state. At the very least we all grow old and sicken. No amount of money can keep that at bay. If we've led lives dedicated only to pleasure, how will we deal with that?

The god worlds hold out great opportunities. But they are very dangerous places as the temptation to give way to mere self-indulgence is always present. It takes a great deal of discipline and determination to handle that situation well.

Maria, like most of us, just passed through the god world for a time. She enjoyed the calm beauty she found there and then used the inspiration she gained to act in the human world once more.

In terms of our experience of money, we touch on the god world when:

- We shop with care and discrimination, buying things only for their genuine aesthetic qualities and not only because of fashion or passing whims.
- Our work itself gives rise to calm, refined mental states.
- We make spending choices that genuinely uplift us, saving to buy really good seats at the theater for example, or for a trip to one of the cultural capitals of Europe.

TRY THIS:

Consider—what is your own version of this kind of experience? Does your work allow you to visit the god realms from time to time? Do you seek out the god world in your leisure time?

What happens when you are in a god world? What causes you to enter it and what causes you to leave it? Does it enhance your creativity, or does it just leave you wanting more pleasure?

## The Human World

The human world is marked by a kind of balance. In it, we experience a certain amount of pleasure and a certain amount of pain. But one of its chief characteristics is that it is a world in which we have a degree of self-awareness and in which we are able to make significant choices. In a human state of mind, we can decide to do things that will be to our own real advantage—or not. The human state, therefore, is one from which we are able to make creative use of the various opportunities that money affords. That choice is not so easily available in some of the other states on the Wheel.

Maria returned to the human world from the god world when she decided to set up her site with some friends to sell art materials on the Web. It's important for humans to have access to the god world from time to time, but if we're seduced into trying to live there we can easily find ourselves slipping into states of inert self-indulgence.

One of the main qualities of the human realm is that it is here that we have most freedom of choice. The gods are given to passive enjoyment, the jealous-gods are driven to succeed, the hungry ghosts are obsessed with their cravings, hell-beings have suffering inflicted on them and animals lack clarity and breadth of mind. If we want to function well in the world of money and make good use of the opportunities it affords, then we need to remain in the human state as much as we are able to.

We know we're in a human state in our relationship to money when:

- ▾ Our financial lives give rise to a mix of pleasure and pain, but we're not overwhelmed by the pain of it nor intoxicated by the pleasure. Instead we continue to make reasonable, clear, informed choices.
- ▾ We enjoy our work *and* our leisure.
- ▾ We form good friendships at work.
- ▾ We're able to forget about money for long periods of time.
- ▾ Our work allows us to grow and develop.
- ▾ We experience twinges of anxiety in relation to money, but we act appropriately and they pass.

- ⁊ We buy what we need and don't feel guilty about it.
- ⁊ We don't obsess about what we want to buy next.
- ⁊ We use our money to come closer to our families, friends, neighbors, the community and the wider world.
- ⁊ What we have is enough.

TRY THIS:

Reflect—what helps you to stay human? Make a list of the things that happen when you're feeling just human. What causes you to enter the human world and what causes you to leave it? What things do you do in the human state that are most central to your life? Can you do them effectively in other states?

⁊  ⁊  ⁊

Were you able to easily complete the exercises in this chapter? Or did you have trouble recognizing what causes you to move from one state to the next? In particular, you might have found it a challenge to know what to do to stay in the human world, or move out of the other five.

The next chapter will give us a deeper understanding of the mechanism that moves us from one state to the next from moment to moment. Once we understand that we'll be in a far better position to exercise choice over where our money-lives lead us. Understanding, and eventually mastering, that mechanism is a key to treading the Path of Abundance.

# TWO

· · · · · · ·

# The Hub and Twelve Links: Bound by the Chains of Desire

What drives the Wheel of Life? Traditional depictions of the Wheel show three animals at the hub—a cock, a snake and a pig—each biting the tail of the one in front. These three animals represent craving, aversion and delusion, and their chasing one another around and around drives the Wheel. Craving, aversion and delusion make the world go round—they are the root cause of our un-Enlightenment and, according to the Buddha, the source of all suffering.

Craving is the desire to possess things that you like, and to include them in your ego-identity in the hope of getting a sense of security from having them as part of you. Aversion is the fearful, angered wish to get rid of things which you dislike and to exclude them from your ego-identity in the hope of attaining a sense of security from *not* having them as part of you. And delusion is the refusal to learn anything that you feel might threaten your ego-identity and upset the sense of security you try to get from it.

Enlightenment, according to the Buddha, consists in the complete eradication of these three unwholesome roots. That is a demanding task. Fortunately, the unwholesome roots are not the whole of our experience. We are also motivated by the three wholesome roots: generosity, kindness and wisdom.

Craving, aversion and delusion keep us trapped in states of narrow self-preoccupation. Generosity, kindness and wisdom are, on the other hand, liberating. They lead to a broader vision of human possibility and are the fundamental basis of a life well-lived.

Only by weakening, and eventually completely transforming the three unwholesome roots, can we become truly creative with money.

Through application and effort, it is possible to escape from the confines of the Wheel altogether and enter fully upon the Path of Abundance. Those who advance along this Path are largely human, although they may visit the god worlds from time to time. They are self-aware—not driven by money matters from world to world, they use money, it doesn't use them. They are responsible, generous and cooperative, using their resources well for their own benefit and that of others. They are independent: not overly concerned with questions of status or acquisition, they are not subject to manipulation. Whether they have a lot or a little, those who tread the Path of Abundance are self-confident, energetic and creative.

All of us can make progress along this Path. Employing just a few of the ideas and exercises outlined in this book, every one of us should soon experience some degree of greater freedom and creativity in relation to money. But to understand the challenge before us, it is worth reflecting for a moment on the history of our collective relationship with craving, aversion and delusion.

## The Boundary of the Self

Once upon a time, many billions of years ago, out of the soup of complex molecules washing about on the Earth, the first ever living organism somehow came together and life as we know it began. This organism had the three fundamental characteristics that it has shared with every succeeding organism over the course of all of the rest of time.

To start with, it had a boundary. If we had been able to transport ourselves and a microscope back through time and we had examined it, we would have been able to say, "Ah yes. An organism. That part inside the boundary is the organism. That part outside isn't."

Second, the organism could take in from the surrounding environment what it needed to survive and it was able, at least for a time, to keep out of the boundary whatever threatened it.

Once you have these three things: a boundary, the ability to take in and the ability to push out, then you have life.

All living organisms do this. They have a more or less stable (but always changing) boundary, and they keep this boundary in place, and thus stay healthy, by taking in what they need and pushing out what threatens them. All living cells do this automatically and the same applies to more complex organisms as well—to frogs, rabbits, elephants and mice. As soon as any organism stops being able to take in what it needs for nourishment and push away whatever threatens it, it dies and is absorbed as food into its environment.

Corporations, cities and nations are like this too. A country that cannot feed and defend itself is eventually absorbed by its more successful neighbors; a corporation that cannot make sufficient profits or protect itself from competitors is soon absorbed by a takeover. And, of course, we humans are subject to the same process. We take in what we want from our environment, we push out what we think threatens us, and so we keep ourselves more or less intact.

We respond to pleasant stimuli with craving and to painful ones with aversion—all the time. "I want this, I don't want that; I like this, I don't like that." We keep doing this from moment to moment, as we respond to the continual flow of change all around us. In this way we constantly make and re-make ourselves, somehow cherishing the delusion that the constantly changing boundary between ourselves and our environment, ourselves and others, can, through those efforts, be kept continuously in place.

Seen in this light, the task of transforming craving, aversion and delusion can seem overwhelming. It's as if there's an unbreakable chain of desire, binding us to the Wheel. How can we do anything about a process that is built so deeply into our essential makeup?

A diamond is the hardest naturally occurring substance on Earth. If we were asked to break one in two, we wouldn't know where to begin. How do you go about breaking something that's the hardest object there is? Skilled diamond cutters know two things. First, they know that you can cut a diamond by using a diamond. In the same way, we break can open the chain of desire by using desire. It all starts with our actively wanting to be free, and so being willing to make the required effort. Second, diamond cutters also know that there are specific points in the structure of the diamond, lines of cleavage, which when struck accurately split the diamond in two. The same applies to the chain of desire. If you know precisely where to apply your effort, the whole process breaks open right in front of you.

## The Twelve-Link Chain

Where is this point in the chain of desire? To see it, we must return to the picture of the Wheel, this time to the outermost circle where there is a series of twelve images. This is actually a twelve-link chain, running around the rim of the Wheel, binding the whole structure together. Between them, these twelve links interact with one another in a process which the Buddha called "dependent arising." In dependence on what happens in the first link, the second link arises. In dependence on what happens in the second link, the third link arises, and so on. Between them, the twelve links form a chain that locks us into the process of cycling from one state to the next, over and over.

There is, however, a weak point in the chain, a spot where we can break free of the process of merely cycling from one state to the next and where we begin to experience a greater degree of freedom and creativity. To get a sense of just where that point is, we need to examine the chain in some detail.

Let's return to the example of Maria. Over the course of a few hours, she touched on each of the six worlds, sometimes more than once. Taking a closer look at some specific moments in her experience we can see that there is a pattern to the process that propelled her from world to world. By understanding that pattern, we can learn to use it to our advantage. This is the first, and perhaps the most important, step along the Path of Abundance.

The twelve-link chain that runs around the rim of the Wheel helps us to understand some of what happened to Maria over that afternoon. Why, for example, did she end up buying yet another pair of shoes?

The first link in the chain is that of *ignorance*, shown in our picture by a blind man, groping his way forward with the help of a stick. The ignorance referred to here isn't the sort of ignorance we have in mind when we think of people who can't name the capital cities of England or the United States or who believe the Earth is flat. It's much deeper than that. It is the spiritual ignorance we all share, the deep-seated belief that if only we had more of what we like and less of what we don't like, then we'd be happy, forever. It also consists in a kind of vagueness about the things that really matter.

Maria, for example, doesn't always know what's good for her. Like many of us, she lives her life more or less instinctively. She gets by from day to day, but she doesn't really know what the meaning of her life is and she can't say that she's really happy or fulfilled. Maybe a raise will make her happier, she sometimes thinks, perhaps a new lover? She doesn't really know and she doesn't ask or know how to ask. She just blindly gropes her way forward through life.

Because she doesn't know what's best for her, her life is usually governed by the next link on the chain, her *habitual impulses*, shown by a potter shaping pots on a wheel. According to the Buddha, the state of spiritual ignorance is rather like drunkenness and our habitual impulses are the actions we perform when we're drunk. They are our unenlightened propensities and under their sway we do, say and think many kinds of things, some of which we might even consider quite wise. But then we've all met drunks who think they're wise. These habitual impulses are the forces that drive us down the well-worn familiar tracks of our lives, the paths of least resistance we've carved as a result of all of our past behavior.

Maria understands a few of her habitual impulses to some extent. She knows, for example, that she has a weakness for buying more shoes than she really needs (her friends call her the Imelda Marcos of cyberspace), and she tries to control the habit, but because she is ignorant of the deeper patterns that govern her behavior she's not able to get completely on top of it. She resolved not to enter the shoe store again but, as we saw, she's not always able to keep her resolutions.

The next link on the chain is *consciousness*, shown by a monkey climbing a flowering tree. The monkey swings from branch to branch, interested now in this flower, now that one. In the same way our ever-changing consciousness swings from world to world, pursuing now this, now that. Our consciousness is never fixed and final, it always changes in dependence on what went before.

In Maria's case, for example, we can see how her past habits made her what she was as she passed by the shop window. Her way of working, for example, sitting for long hours in front of her screen, absorbed in writing computer code, left her in a numbed, animal state of mind. She had "programmer's consciousness"—a slightly anesthetized, abstracted state of mind. That consciousness was the result of the acts that had immediately preceded it.

Next on the chain comes *the psychophysical organism*, shown by a boat and with four passengers, one of whom is steering. The boat represents bodily form, and the passengers represent feeling, perception, volition and consciousness (which steers the boat). These are the five factors which, the Buddha said, made up a human being. We are, he added, just an assembly of these factors—a constantly changing arrangement of changing processes, shaped and re-shaped by what we do.

When Maria passed by the shoe store she had spent hours locked on to her screen. That produced programmer's consciousness, as we've seen, which affected her body, making her stiff and slightly achy; her feelings, which were slightly numbed; her perception, which was dulled; and her volitions, which were unconscious and habitual as she was barely aware of them. Consciousness comes first—everything else follows.

The next link in the chain is that of *the six sense organs* (mind being the sixth sense in Buddhism). This is shown on the Wheel by a house with five windows and a door. The way our sense organs function, what they tell us about the world, depends on what went before. After hours of programming, Maria's senses were dulled.

In her blurred state of mind she passed by the shoe store. If she'd been more alert she'd have noticed more. She might have enjoyed the smell of a fresh spring day, the laughter of kids in a playground, the first faint feeling of spring sun on her skin. She might have noticed and thought about the man slumped on the sidewalk outside the store. But she didn't. Her senses were functioning in a dull, habit-ridden kind of way and that conditioned what came next.

She glanced in the window, and saw a pair of shoes. The moment when the shoes registered in her mind is shown in the next link, a couple embracing. This stands for *contact*. Out of the myriad possibilities of sense experience in that moment, Maria's senses focused upon a pair of shoes. If her boyfriend had been passing with her by the same window he'd not have noticed them at all. He would, in a way, have been experiencing quite a different world from Maria's, with other preoccupations. Perhaps he'd have been wondering about the likely outcome of a ball game that night—his team was really starting to get somewhere. Or maybe he was more interested in the all-terrain bike in the window next door. What our senses incline toward, the world they present to us, the contact we have with it, is conditioned by all that went before in our lives.

"Shoes!" thought Maria, and as a result of that contact, and because of her past habitual impulses, certain *feelings* arose in her. This is the next link on the chain and is shown by a man with an arrow in his eye.

Every moment of contact we have with the world comes with an associated feeling tone—pleasant, painful or neutral. In this case, the shoes in the window gave Maria a strong set of pleasant feelings. "*Nice* shoes!"

Wanting those feelings to continue, she arrived at the next link in the chain: *craving*. This is depicted by a woman offering a drink to a seated man.

Pleasant feelings give rise to craving in us, unpleasant ones to aversion, and neutral ones to bewilderment (we don't know *what* we feel). We respond with desire or dislike to whatever set off our feelings in the first place and, acting on that, we move on to the next link in the chain—*grasping*, we reach out to get what we want. This is symbolized by the image of a person picking fruit off a tree.

Despite her resolve not to buy yet another pair of shoes that month, Maria turned into the store, sat down and tried them on. She walked up and down a bit and asked the salesperson's opinion. ("Well, I think they look just great on you—they're kind of your color, you know.") She took them off, paused, put them on again, walked about, twirled, and made up her mind. "They'll be perfect with those new linen pants!" She took out her credit card and bought them, but somehow the feeling of pleasure that she expected from her purchase never quite came. She was left with a niggling feeling of dissatisfaction.

That is because of what had now happened, and it is marked by the link of *becoming*, symbolized by a pregnant woman. Maria left home in an animal state of mind, her experience in the shoe shop propelled her into another world for a time. She became a hungry ghost. The chain of desire had moved her from one state to another. Every time we act, a new state of mind, a new situation—a new world, even—arises.

But Maria didn't stay in the hungry ghost world for long. In the gym, because of her workout, she became human again—so when she got home and looked at the shoes, she wondered what had come over her. This movement from one world to the next is marked by the last two links in the chain. Here we see a woman giving birth and a man carrying a corpse to the charnel ground. These stand simply and starkly for *birth* and *death*. Situations arise and pass away, over and over. We just seem to keep circling around the Wheel, blindly driven by craving and aversion from one state to the next.

## The Creative Opportunity

If there were no alternative to circling about the Wheel, passing from state to state with no real choice about where we end up, life would be pretty bleak. Fortunately, it isn't all like this. There is a weak point in the chain, a tiny opening which, if we attend closely, turns out to be an opening to freedom. That point is where the link of feeling gives way to the link of craving. There, what comes from the past intersects with the present and we can decide to act differently. At this point of opportunity we can consciously choose to take ourselves off in a creative direction. It is the opening to the Path of Abundance. Once we learn how to identify that point we can begin actively to seek it out and make opportunities to progress along that Path all the time.

Maria happened upon the link between feeling and craving several times in her afternoon but was able to turn it into a creative opening just once. After she'd lost her temper and stormed out of her apartment, she marched down to the park and strode around the lake, fuming, when suddenly a clump of bright yellow flowers caught her eye and she stopped and stared.

Up until then, all of Maria's actions had been more or less "reactive." She saw the shoes and reacted with craving, she got an e-mail from Tony and reacted with aversion. These reactions drove her around and around on the Wheel. Even now, she could have responded with craving to the pleasant feelings that the flowers produced in her. She might have picked one and continued to cycle around the Wheel, but she didn't. Instead she somehow managed to stay with her pleasant feelings and just attend to them. Because she gave so much attention to her feelings, she didn't move on to the next link in the Wheel. Instead, she entered a wide-open space. Her awareness blossomed and she leaned on the railings, watched the gull wheeling in the sky. Suffused with calm, she enjoyed the pure pleasure of simply being in the moment.

In her clear, refined, aware, godlike state, Maria was less driven by the central motive force of the Wheel. With craving and aversion somewhat abated, it became possible for her to make a free choice about what to do with her future. Rather than reactive, she became, for a time at least, creative, and she happened upon an exciting new way to make her living.

She started her new company in a small way, not borrowing very much, so when the dotcom bubble burst she was able to keep going. She now employs five people and the company has made it into the black. She expects she'll have time for her painting some time next year.

## Learning to Make Creative Choices

The move from reactivity to creativity is the first step along the Path of Abundance. This process has two components, one negative (in the sense of not doing), one positive. The first component is learning not to react. The second component, which we will examine when we look at the final circle of the Wheel, involves learning how to act skillfully.

Maria came upon the practice of nonreactivity almost accidentally. But it doesn't have to be accidental. We can consciously set out to cultivate a less reactive attitude, and there are a variety of ways of training ourselves in the practice.

The basis of nonreactivity is learning to work in the gap between feeling and craving (or aversion). It's important to discriminate here between our basic feelings and the more complex emotions that follow from them. Our basic feelings, as we're using the term here, are the simple responses we have to sensations. Every sensation gives rise to a certain feeling tone, and these basic feelings are pleasant, painful or neutral. Emotions are much more complex than this. Negative emotions have elements of craving, aversion or delusion mixed up in them; positive ones are marked by the presence of generosity, love or clarity. But whether they're positive or negative, emotions are active responses to our more basic feelings. They are something we can actually *choose*.

Imagine you're sitting in your living room at home, and smells of cooking come wafting in from the kitchen. At first, what you experience is the simple sensation: cooking smells. Then you register these as pleasant, unpleasant or neutral. If they're pleasant, your mind will incline toward them—you'll want to get more involved with them. If they're unpleasant, you'll shy away from them; and if they're neutral, you'll probably ignore them. Now, if the feeling tone associated with the smell sensation is pleasant, you'll begin to crave your dinner—you'll start to entertain the thought of food, becoming imaginatively involved in it. "Mmmm . . . roast pota-toes. I wonder when they'll be ready. . . ." The fact that you find the smell of roasting potatoes pleasant comes from how you've lived in the past. If you were forced to eat them every day when you were a child, perhaps you'd find the same smell unpleasant. Because our response of pleasure or pain comes from the past, there's noth-ing we can do about it right now. But when our minds incline toward a pleasant sensation and we get involved in it, then we're actively doing something in the present, and we can, if we wish, choose not to. You could, if you were on a diet and were disci-plined, think "Mmm . . . roast potatoes. They smell good. But they're not for me." And you could not fall into craving them. Crav-ing is something we *choose* to do.

Let's look again at this segment of the Wheel. We experience something (contact), we like it (pleasant feeling), we crave it (emo-tion) and we reach out for it (grasping). Because of all she did in the past, pleasant feelings inevitably arose in Maria when she saw the shoes. She then began to crave them, and that was a conscious ac-tion—and one she need not have done. In a way that was barely dis-cernible to her, she made a micro-decision to crave those shoes.

## Taking Control of Our Micro-Decisions

There is this tiny moment of choice in all of us that precedes the onset of craving or aversion. This fact is so important that it bears repeating. Craving is not something that just happens to us. It is something we *do*.

If we want to gain some control over this cycle in ourselves and enter the Path of Abundance, we need to broaden the moment of choice that exists between feeling and craving. We do that by culti-vating a greater degree of overall awareness. Imagine, for example, that you are in an art gallery and you see a great painting that really moves you. It's possible to stand there, in front of the picture, and just enjoy the delightful feelings that the picture produces in you. You can revel in the higher level of awareness that a great picture can produce in you—or you can get involved in wanting to own the art yourself. But once you do the latter, you will have moved around the Wheel and crossed the gap between feeling and craving. You will also have lost the living awareness of the beauty of the picture. As you get involved in craving, the direct experience of beauty slips into the past. It becomes a memory rather than a current experience.

By cultivating a higher degree of overall awareness, by learning to enjoy the process simply of being aware, we can learn to stay in that gap for longer, living in the present, right here and now, fully alive to the world all about us.

To begin, we need to identify, and learn to stay with, our basic feelings.

TRY THIS:
Stop here and consider your present experience, as you are reading this book, wherever you are. What is its basic feeling tone—pleasant, unpleasant or indifferent? Try to sense that basic feeling tone, separate from the thoughts and emotions that are currently taking place in your mind.

The way we live our lives today, it's not always easy to tell whether our current experience is pleasant, painful or neutral. But don't worry—just sit still and "listen" to your overall experience. Bring your attention to your body, particularly your overall physical posture. Experience the tension or relaxation in your muscles and the overall flow of your physical energy. Become aware of your breathing, and follow your breath for a few moments. In this way, you will gradually become more aware of your basic feelings, pleasant or painful. Don't worry if your awareness is weak at first. Our basic feelings can be quite subtle but so long as we're aware of them, even just a little aware, then we can work with them.

Once you're aware of your basic feelings, watch how pleasant feelings incline your mind to craving, unpleasant ones incline it to aversion. Now, see if you can tell how you make that tiny micro-decision to get involved with craving or aversion.

Remember the example of the cooking smells. We can sit there simply enjoying the pleasant aromas, or we can slip into wanting the food. The decision is ours. Can you see, in your own experience, how you make those decisions?

Let's look at a few alternate scenarios in which Maria might have acted differently in the course of that afternoon. Maybe she decided that her way of working in front of her screen without a break was doing her no good, so she took the experts' advice and had regular breaks through the course of her day. She took her lunch in the park, making a point of just sitting quietly, coming back to her feelings and enjoying the sight of the trees and the clouds. Perhaps, too, she stopped work for a few moments every forty-five minutes, got up and walked around—poured a drink, looked out the window and stretched her body. As a result of all this, when she passed the shoe store on her way to the gym she was feeling relatively human. She caught sight of the shoes, and enjoyed their sleek design. "Nice shoes," she thought, "but I don't need another pair." She made the micro-decision not to crave them.

When she got back home and clicked on e-mail, she read Tony's rather blunt message. "Hmm . . . ," she thought. "That Tony again . . . I must get over to the office some time, take him out for a coffee and find a way of talking to him about his manner." She made the micro-decision not to give way to aversion.

Maria was able to make these creative micro-decisions because she was more in touch with her feelings and more aware of her overall state of mind. Practice returning to your feelings from time to time in the course of the day. By developing a stronger and more continuous awareness of our feelings we can work more creatively in the gap between feeling and craving (or aversion). So, for example:

▾ You pass by a bakery. You've made a resolution to eat less sugar and fat, but the Sacher torte looks so inviting. . . . Breathe, check out your feelings. By identifying and staying with our feelings in such circumstances we remain in charge of the situation. We don't blindly give way and find ourselves, regretfully, having eaten a huge piece of cake before we've even thought what we're doing.

▾ On the subway, you reach into your back pocket for your wallet and it's missing. Don't panic. Pause. Take three breaths, stay with the unpleasant feeling. Okay, now you're set to act appropriately.

▾ There's a note on your desk, your boss wants to see you. He has been firing people all week. Stop. Check out your body. How are you feeling? Stay with that, keep with your feelings as they change, don't lose it, and you'll know just what to say when you meet him. As the meeting unfolds, check out your body from time to time. It helps to keep you grounded in your feelings—and helps you not to act out of panic and fear.

TRY THIS:

1. Set aside a period of time in the course of your day, perhaps a few hours, when you're going to make a particular effort to watch out for those micro-decisions you make where feelings pass over into craving or aversion. Remind yourself that it's your decision to crave. It's something you do and it's something you can take responsibility for. See if you can catch yourself doing it. Try to make a different decision instead.

2. Think about a habitual craving you would like to change. If you like chocolate cake, can you experience the pleasant sight of a slice without wanting to buy it? Try sitting with the pleasant feeling that normally gives way to that craving and don't go over the edge—just experience the pleasant

feelings as pleasant in themselves. See if you can simply sit, enjoying those feelings for a time. Do you find the craving dies away?

## Taking Control of Our Macro-Decisions

Once we have begun to get some familiarity with the process by which we make the reactive micro-decisions in our lives, the process whereby we move from experiencing something, to enjoying and then craving it (or not enjoying it and therefore feeling aversion toward it), then we will be in a much better position to take control of the significant macro-decisions we make that between them determine the overall direction of our lives.

We can live somewhat purposelessly, cycling around the Wheel, driven by craving and aversion from one state to the next, over and over, or we can live purposefully, treading the Path of Abundance, aware of our goals and orientation. How we do that, we shall see in detail in the following chapters.

# THREE

## The Black and White Segments: Taking Charge of Your Life

We'd all like to be more creative. We'd all like to free ourselves from the Wheel. And yet . . . The chains of desire are so strong. How can we ever break them? As we saw earlier, a diamond cutter uses a diamond to cut a diamond. If we want to break the chains of desire, we have to use something equally strong. We use desire.

There are two kinds of desire. There is reactive desire, that keeps us trapped on the Wheel, and there is creative desire, the pursuit of what is good, true or beautiful, that leads us off the Wheel and into states of increased freedom. The art of decreasing the first kind of desire and increasing the second kind of desire involves a training in what Buddhists call "skillfulness," and just what that entails we shall discover as we explore the final segment of the Wheel.

The second from the middle circle of the Wheel is divided into two segments, one black, one white. In the white segment, beings rise upward, toward states of greater happiness. In the black one they plunge downward into painful states. This circle shows how what we consciously do affects us. It illustrates the principles upon which all of Buddhist ethics are based.

How should we act? What will make us happy? What is the right thing to do? If you want to be happy, the Buddha said, and move toward Enlightenment, then you should train yourself in ethical conduct.

He once addressed a gathering of his monks. "Monks," he said, "when you act well there is no need to think 'May I become free from remorse.' This is simply in accordance with nature—for one who acts well, freedom from remorse arises. And when you are free from remorse, there is no need to think 'May joy arise in me.' Again, it accords with nature—in one who is free from remorse joy arises. And when you are joyous, there is no need to think 'May rapture arise in me.' It is completely natural. For in one who is joyous rapture arises."

So he went on, unfolding the stages of a path that proceeded through ever more creative mental states. Rapture gives rise to profound calm, that leads to deep happiness, meditative concentration follows, and as a result, one becomes disentangled from things, and so one becomes Enlightened.

"Thus," he said, "one state just causes the next state to swell, one state causes the fulfillment of another state, for the sake of going from un-Enlightenment to Enlightenment."[9]

The earlier stages of this path are easy enough for us to see in our own experience. If we act well, we grow free from remorse. That's pretty clear, and if we're free from remorse we experience a kind of innocent delight in things, a kind of joy. Maybe we've all touched on that joy from time to time. If we experience it more than fleetingly, delight can intensify into rapture.

Perhaps at this point the Buddha's teaching is starting to surpass

---

9. Anguttara Nikaya, *The Book of the Tens.*

our own immediate experience. But the basic principle of his path is pretty clear, and starts with how we act. That is why we train ourselves ethically—for the sake of going from un-Enlightenment to Enlightenment.

Imagine being fully, completely loving, generous, contented, honest and aware. That (as we'll see a bit later) is Enlightenment, and that is the goal of Buddhist ethics. To begin with Enlightenment can seem somewhat abstract and distant, but by trying to put Buddhist ethical teachings into practice in our daily lives, from moment to moment, we learn more and more about the realities of the goal and of the path to achieving it. In the process of doing so, we come into an ever-better relationship to others and to the world we live in.

Buddhism does not speak in terms of "good" and "bad" behavior. No act, according to Buddhist thought, is good or bad in itself. Instead they are skillful or unskillful. Skillful or unskillful at what? you may ask. At the task of moving toward Enlightenment, which is the ultimate aim of the Buddhist life.

Skillful acts bring us nearer to the goal of Enlightenment. As we have seen, the boundary between ourselves and others, ourselves and the world, is actually a fiction. It's something we keep in place through our repeated acts of craving, aversion and delusion. Skillful acts come from a deeper sense of the interrelation of all things. They accord with the way things really are, and they always bring about beneficial results. They are, in other words, creative.

Unskillful acts, on the other hand, are based in excessive self-concern and a desire to maintain the boundary between ourselves and the world. They take us further away from the goal of Enlightenment, cause us to rub up against reality in painful ways and bring about states of lonely isolation. Since they are our blind reactions to feelings of pleasure or pain, we also call them reactive.

## What Karma Really Means

According to the Buddha, what makes any act skillful or unskillful is the motive which underlies it. Karma literally means "willed act" and the Buddha taught that there is a "law of karma," a natural law, not unlike our law of gravity, according to which acts based in kindly intentions always have beneficial consequences whereas acts rooted in selfish motives always have painful consequences. It all comes down to intention. Why?

CONSIDER THESE DIFFERENT SCENARIOS—

Jim grabs a sandwich from a sandwich bar for his lunch. The smallest bill he has is a fifty and he receives two twenties and a five in his change. He puts them in his billfold, leaves the coins as a tip, and goes back to work. One of the twenties is counterfeit, but Jim's a little nearsighted and doesn't notice. On the way home that evening he stops for some groceries, the shopkeeper accepts the fake twenty and Jim knows no more about it.

Now rewind the tape and play a different scenario from the point where Jim gets his change. As he takes the cash from the person at the counter, he feels that there's something a little odd about the bottom twenty. The texture of the paper isn't quite right, but he's in a rush to return to work so he stuffs the notes into his billfold and heads back to the office.

That afternoon, a friend in the office passes by. "Hey, Jim," he says, "check your wallet. Someone in the neighborhood's been passing off fake twenties."

Jim has a dim recollection of feeling that something wasn't quite right with his change. "No," he thinks. "Forget that. Too much hassle." And so in a state of willful ignorance he just lets things lie. On the way home he spends the twenty on groceries. But he didn't do that knowingly. Well, not altogether knowingly.

Rewind again. His friend warns him about the counterfeit bill and Jim recollects that sense that there was something wrong with his change. He leafs through his billfold and comes to the twenty. Yes, it's a counterfeit bill. After thinking about it for a while, he decides to pass it on as soon as he can. He needs some groceries, so on the way home he selects a shop where he knows there will be a new immigrant behind the till. He makes his purchases, hands over the twenty and collects his change.

Now rewind again to the point where Jim leafs through his billfold and spots the counterfeit bill. He sighs. "Oh, well—win a few, lose a few." On the way home from work he stops in at the local precinct and hands the fake bill to the officer behind the desk. Then he heads off to buy some groceries.

What kind of person does Jim become as a result of the way in which he handles the fake twenty in each of these episodes?

In the first episode, he unknowingly spends the fake bill on groceries. The act of handing over the counterfeit twenty on this occasion is karmically neutral. Neither Jim nor his own immediate world is changed much by it.

In the second episode, Jim again hands the note to a person in a grocery store. Although he doesn't realize it, his ignorance now is willful, because he deliberately ignored his friend's warning, and to that extent his action is karmically somewhat negative. Like many of us, he prefers not to face up to some ethical difficulties. As a result, the world he inhabits is vague at the edges. He is less clear than he could be, slightly unaware of himself and his environment, and things tend to go wrong for him again and again. He's not looking where he's going. But there's more to it than that. The suffering people inflict upon one another comes about, not merely through the malevolent acts of single individuals, but also through the willful ignorance of those who would otherwise do good.

In the third episode, the act of using the fake twenty as payment for groceries, the selfsame physical act but with a different motive, is karmically much more negative. By willingly deceiving the shop-keeper Jim strengthens his own tendency to selfishness and deceit-fulness. He becomes more likely to act deceitfully in the future as the habit of doing so is made stronger. The niggling sense he has of being somewhat isolated and cutoff from others is reinforced and his world becomes that little bit bleaker and more apparently hostile as his encounters with others are colored by his self-preoccuption.

In the fourth episode Jim hands over the twenty again, this time to a police officer, and, financially at least, he loses out. But karmic-ally his action is much more positive. Acting honestly and ethically, Jim becomes a bit less selfish. His world opens out a little more, it becomes lighter and brighter, and his relationships with others go on more easily as people sense that he is the kind of man they can trust.

In Buddhist terms, handing a counterfeit bill to someone else is neither good nor bad in itself. What made the chief difference in each of these episodes was the motive underlying the act.

Karmic results happen in the same way that apples fall off trees under the influence of gravity—they are part of the natural order. As humans, we are neither intrinsically good nor bad. But we do have choice. At every moment we can chose to act skillfully or un-skillfully—creatively or reactively. When we have completed train-ing in skillful living we become like highly trained artists or athletes—skillful choices then come to us naturally and sponta-neously. Until then, however, certain rules of training are really useful, even essential.

## The Five Precepts

The Buddha taught a basic framework to help guide our conduct. If you want to be happy, he said, and move toward Enlightenment, then you should train yourself as follows—

- ▾ Refrain from taking life
- ▾ Don't take what hasn't been freely given to you
- ▾ Avoid sexual misconduct
- ▾ Don't lie
- ▾ Refrain from intoxication

These "five precepts" are practiced throughout the Buddhist world and, as we shall see when we look at each of them in detail in the following chapters, they all have a significant economic dimension.

These precepts may seem to require us simply to refrain from certain activities. But that is not enough. Were we able successfully to do that, it might deal with the reactive tendency in our nature, but it would not, alone, make us more creative. As well as reducing our unskillfulness, we should also cultivate skillfulness.

We can think of every precept as having a positive counterpart. For instance, we don't just refrain from taking life—we also cultivate loving-kindness. (We'll discuss each precept in turn in later chapters.) Our practice of the precepts isn't a rote exercise that we do purely out of shame and guilt. Rather, it is expansive and joyful. We give up confined, self-preoccupied mental states and replace them with expansive, joyful and generous ones. We give up the less for the sake of the more because what we could become, with practice, is so much more inviting than what we now are. Good conduct leads to freedom from remorse. Freedom from remorse leads to joy, joy leads to rapture, then to calm, happiness, concentration and finally to Enlightenment.

## Right Livelihood

The Buddha placed great emphasis in his teaching on the way people earn their living. There is wrong livelihood, he said, and right livelihood. How do we find our right livelihood? Among committed Western Buddhists there are a number of alternatives. A small minority take formal monastic ordination and some of these live off alms. Others try to find congenial work where their Buddhist values are taken into account and they have space for their practice. Some try simply to do as little work as possible, maximizing their income per hour worked and/or minimizing their expenses so as to allow time for what they value more. Some seek out vocational work—teaching, health care, social work and so on that allows them to express their Buddhist values in daily life. Others opt for a kind of damage control working in a noncongenial environment but trying to keep their involvement with it to a minimum. Some try to earn as much as possible, in order to enhance their capacity for generosity or to allow them to retire early, and some have tried to work out more collective solutions to the issue, joining freestanding Buddhist enterprises. But the teaching of right livelihood enjoins all of these—everyone—in their own ways, to make how they earn and spend an aspect of their Buddhist practice.

In the Parable of the Medicinal Herbs, found in the Lotus Sutra, the Buddha tells his followers that his teaching is for everyone. It is like rain that falls on all plants alike.

> The rain falls everywhere,
> coming down on all four sides.
> Its flow and saturation are measureless,
> reaching to every area of the earth,
> to the ravines and valleys of the mountains and streams,
> to the remote and secluded places where grow
> plants, bushes and medicinal herbs,
> trees large and small,
> a hundred grains, rice seedlings,
> sugar cane, grape vines.
> The rain moistens them all,
> none fails to receive its fair share.

*The parched ground is everywhere watered,*
*herbs and trees alike grow lush.*
*What falls from the cloud is water of a single flavor,*
*but the plants and trees, thickets and groves,*
*each accepts the moisture that is appropriate to its portion. . . .*[10]

The rain in this parable is the refreshing rain of truth and we are the plants. But every plant, every one of us, is different and so, as the rain falls on us, we grow in different ways.

We all have to practice the teachings in our own ways and according to our own circumstances, and the five precepts are our guide. Accurate statistics are hard to come by, but by now there must be hundreds of thousands of Buddhists in the West actively striving to put the principles of right livelihood into practice in their everyday lives. How some of them are doing that, how Buddhists follow the Five Precepts as they earn, spend, give and invest we will examine in greater detail as we embark upon the Path of Abundance.

---

10. Translated by Burton Watson, *The Lotus Sutra* (New York: Columbia University Press, 1993), p. 101.

# PART TWO

# The Path of
Abundance

# FOUR

## The First Precept: Cultivate Loving-Kindness

*Don't harm living beings, instead cultivate kindness.*

What's the most harmful thing that you can do? For a Buddhist, as in other belief-systems, it's taking life. Killing is the most extreme way of declaring ourselves separate from the rest of the world, and more important than anything within it. But short of taking life, there are many ways to harm: by causing pain or by restricting life's possibilities. There are also many ways to expand the magical possibilities that being alive can offer us all.

Much of this has to do with our earning and spending. In this chapter, we start to explore the Path of Abundance by unraveling the consequences of how we spend. We'll learn less harmful, more skillful ways of going about it. Key to this effort is awakening our imagination to help us see, then closing the gaps between ourselves, others and the world.

## Understanding the Consequences
## of How We Spend

In this vast interconnected global economy, our purchases always have unexpected consequences. If you use your car, or even take a bus, to go shopping, you pump out greenhouse gases. The food you buy at the supermarket has been sprayed with insecticides and herbicides that damage the environment and is wrapped in non-biodegradable packaging. The white T-shirt you wear was bleached perhaps in Hungary and the run-off from the mill is doing no good to the country's freshwater fish. When we turn on a light switch in Britain, we place that much more demand on the national power grid and so help to pour acid rain on Sweden from the sulfurous by-products of the fossil fuels burned in power stations.

Even when we make a particular effort not to harm others, it's not always easy. The totally non-leather, vegetarian-option sneakers that some of our friends try so hard to find may be made under appalling sweatshop conditions in South East Asia. Almost everything we do in the economic sphere creates some harm somewhere. With the best will in the world, it's hard to spend even fifty cents without doing some damage.

In the face of this fact, one creative response is to learn more about the likely consequences of our economic behavior, and develop a real appetite to limit the damage that we do.

Let's look at meat. It doesn't arrive on our plates without animals being killed, and many Buddhists in the West simply won't touch it. The point of the first precept, however, is not that Buddhism has forbidden meat eating. Buddhist precepts are not commandments: they are training principles, ways to help us learn about ourselves in relation to the world. Here's an example.

Suzanne has fast-growing kids. She's well aware that they need plenty of protein in their diet and they just won't eat tofu. She buys them meat, but she's taken the trouble to check out the different butchers in her local area, and talk to them about their sources. The guy at the supermarket had no idea where his cuts came from, so Suzanne gave his counter a miss. It didn't take her long to find a supplier who had taken pains to ensure as humane a means of slaughter as Suzanne could reasonably expect. The butcher was quite a lot more expensive than the supermarket alternative, but Suzanne had thought through how much protein the kids really needed and that was leading her to buy rather less meat anyway. Similarly, she knows that the antibiotics that she took last month were tested on animals. She's chosen to do a little bit of harm for her health's sake, but not for her looks: she won't buy animal-tested cosmetics. She's learning to make conscious, considered choices, understanding more and more how she relates to the world and engaging with it wholeheartedly. Others might make different choices: there is no one way.

One of our friends was urging us to be prescriptive. "We've got to stop low-wage labor exploitation in the developing world. People who call themselves Buddhist," he told us firmly, "have got to join the Nike boycott." We did not agree. A boycott might give our sense of righteous indignation some exercise, and we ourselves might feel better as a result, but for all we know, it could cause even greater harm to workers to whom any job, however ill-paid, is precious. We need to be curious and concerned enough to investigate the issue, recognize its complexity and work out our own point of view. And then we need to be responsible enough to act on it, whether it pleases or dismays our friends. We wouldn't tell anyone to join an ethical boycott, nor would we tell anyone not to. We each have to develop our own ethical potency by figuring out what to do.

It's the same with a seemingly ethical product like Fair Trade coffee. If we just sweep the Fair Trade packs off the shelf as a ritual act of goodness, it doesn't help us learn much about the relationship between the coffee growers and ourselves. But if we occasionally reflect on the lives of those who picked the beans as we sip our morning coffee, wonder what it's like to be them and consciously act to improve the conditions that they live in, then we've begun to learn about causing less harm. We'll achieve an awakening and re-orientation of self in relation to others with consequences going far beyond the improvement of peasant coffee grower profit margins, important as that is.

As more and more of us intensify our engagement with the world in this way, we'll influence our friends, our families and our co-workers so we'll all learn to limit the harm that we do. Often, the pressure for companies to limit harm comes less from lobbyists than from their employees' desire to have something to be proud of when they go home.

Let's consider how we might learn to harm the environment less. Almost anyone reading this book knows how easily we damage it. Choosing a place to live that entails a lengthy commute; owning a large, gas-guzzling vehicle (or several) for the family to ride in; not using public transportation where it's available: these are just a start. And yet, how do we learn to limit these abuses, or encourage others to do less environmental harm? We might issue our environmentally destructive neighbors with a list of environmentally responsible injunctions. "Travel less!" "Ride the bus!" "Switch off lights!" "Eat organic!" "Recycle now!" But will they? People don't change their behavior through being told what to do. Changing our behavior is an outcome of learning: we learn enough to make us curious about an alternative state of being; as we learn more it starts to seduce us; as we practice it, the practice arouses our imagination and then we start to extend the practice into our lives.

## DAMAGE CONTROL IN SPENDING

How can you limit the amount of damage you do? If you're not already doing so, in what ways could you implement any of the following suggestions?

- ▾ Choose a place to live that reduces the need to drive.
- ▾ Choose a fuel-efficient, low-pollution car.
- ▾ Try to reduce the amount you travel.
- ▾ Where possible, walk, cycle, or use public transportation.
- ▾ Eat less meat, or none at all.
- ▾ Buy organic produce.
- ▾ Choose a low-energy home.
- ▾ Install energy-efficient lighting, heating and other appliances.
- ▾ Choose an electricity supplier who offers energy from renewable sources.
- ▾ Reduce your consumption, re-use and recycle.
- ▾ Seek Fair Trade producers where possible.
- ▾ Prefer local produce and products that have not been tested on live animals.

What other changes could you implement? What makes it difficult for you to do some of these things?

## Awakening the Kindly Imagination

How does learning begin? How do we find a way into the behavior that we want to alter? Take the excessive use of private transportation. Rather than lecturing ourselves and inducing, briefly, a little guilt, we might get a hold of a bicycle, and go for a ride on a glorious spring weekend day. Then we might try riding it to work once in a while. Again, it's wise to pick a sunny day outside the rush hour to get us going, but sooner or later we'll wake up to the impact of exhaust fumes in our nostrils, and congested roads that leave us perilously close to swaying trucks. Then we'll know what excessive use of private transport means for the environment, and have a real desire to limit it, because we've learned that the environment is intimately connected with our own self. We need to bring what we harm to life imaginatively. As our imagination is kindled, we'll be seduced into an appreciation for what we're harming. And that appreciation will cause us to experience at least some faint echo of the pain that we're inflicting, so we'll seek to inflict less.

In creative ways like this, we can learn to make our consumption less harmful. But in the end there is no escaping the world as it is. We can't all go off and become self-sufficient hermits (if there is such a thing) and nothing is gained through becoming economically inert. All that does is paralyze us. Instead we need to engage with the world of money in such a way as to try, however we can, to help more than we harm. We have the power to put the balance right. Through our earning and spending we can transform the world with kindness.

Acts of kindness spring from the realization that we don't have to be mean-spirited, self-enclosed creatures; that in the end, it's an illusion to see ourselves as separate from the rest of the world. The root of kindness is a rich, imaginative identification with others: by practicing the first precept we learn to bring about others' joys and feel them as our own.

It's easy to underestimate our capacity for kindness. Small acts ripple outward and have unexpected effects. In the aftermath of the attack on the World Trade Center, the writer Stephen Jay Gould wrote about how his wife and stepdaughter set up a depot on Spring Street to ferry much needed items to the rescue workers at Ground Zero. Word of what they were doing spread and all kinds of donations poured in, from a pocketful of batteries to $10,000 worth of hard hats spontaneously purchased at a local store.

As the Goulds left a nearby restaurant late one evening on their way to make a delivery, the cook came up to them with a shopping bag. "Here's a dozen apple brown Bettys, our very best dessert. They're still warm. Please give them to the rescue workers." How lovely, thought Gould, but how meaningless, except as a symbolic act of solidarity. They promised to deliver them and put the bag on top of several thousand face masks and shoe inserts. Twelve apple brown Bettys and thousands of rescue workers.

The brown Bettys went like hotcakes. They gave the last to a firefighter, one of the older men in a young crowd who sat alone, exhausted, as he inserted one of their shoe-pads. His face brightened and a smile returned to his face. "Thank you," he said. "That's the loveliest thing I've seen in four days. And it's still warm."

What Gould had thought of as a trivial gesture had turned into a drop of gold. A stranger stopped being a stranger: the gap between self and other had narrowed.

## Closing the Gaps Between Self, Other and the World

Closing the gap between self and other, between humanity and the world, has to be a central preoccupation for the times in which we now live. Not so long ago, we really could avoid each other. Impoverished communities on the far side of the planet with strange, even abhorrent religions and customs could be invisible and ignored. But now, they see us all too clearly. They see our extraordinary wealth, our encouragement of values and behaviors that strike at the heart of what they care for most. And we now see them. Our globalized economy brought us so much closer; through global travel, global media, global brands. But that was a physical closeness only. The distance in terms of human understanding and empathy remains breathtakingly vast.

Closing the gap between self and other is a central aspiration of Buddhism, and Buddhist practitioners have developed a range of powerful techniques to help them do so. Of these, Buddhists regard meditation as particularly important. Meditation works directly on the mind, and the mind governs our actions. When we meditate, we use the mental space that otherwise gets used for fantasy or day-

dreaming in a conscious and potent way. A classic meditation practice that has been taught across the Buddhist world for over two
thousand years is called the "Development of Loving-Kindness." It
provides rich insights about ways in which we can develop kindness
when we're not meditating, as well as when we're sitting on the
meditation mat.

In this meditation practice we start by being kind to ourselves.
This is akin to the notion that "charity begins at home," because it's
generally easier to do a kindness to ourselves than to anyone else.
Not only that: it's essential to begin with ourselves, because if you
can't love yourself, you won't be able to love others. And so, sitting
relaxed and comfortable with our eyes closed, we would direct
thoughts of loving-kindness to ourselves. There are many ways to
do this. You might imagine yourself carried away to a particularly
beautiful place, or surrounded by light of a really beautiful color.
You might recall a time when you were particularly happy, and remember the setting, the people, even the smell of the place as
vividly as possible. You could search within yourself for some flicker
of happiness that's already there and give it more and more of your
attention: it might be a sense of warmth around the heart that you
could fan gently with the breath. Or you might simply turn over
and over in your mind the words "May I be happy, may I be well,
may I be free from suffering." And as you made that wish, you'd take
note of how it felt, allowing any feelings of warmth, peace and joy
to expand. The point here is not primarily to feel happy, so much
as to experience what it's like to wish ourselves happiness. It's the
wishing that is the act of kindness.

That's just to get started: this practice will take us far beyond
ourselves. Many of us today lead rather isolated, self-enclosed lives.
This practice can help us awaken to the truth of interdependence,
that we all depend upon one another in many ways, and it can help
us to generate the strong positive emotions that make for a life lived
skillfully within the context of community.

We begin with our self because it's our natural tendency to

look after ourselves very well indeed. That's a fact. It is pointless to tell ourselves "Be selfless!" The practice of loving-kindness teaches us to recognize our capacity for self-love, build on it and transform it progressively. That means moving, step by step, from easier assignments to tougher ones. So, the next target for our capacity to be kind is a really good friend. This is someone toward whom we can easily feel warmth. We might imagine how delighted we'd be if this friend were sitting with us while we were meditating, or reflect on why we take such pleasure in this person's company, or remember the specific ways in which this friend has been kind to us. And you could imagine your friend in a beautiful place, in a situation that makes her really happy and so on. In your mind, you could turn over the words "May she be happy!" and see what actual feelings of kindness start to spread.

Raising the stakes a bit more, you next conjure up in your mind somebody for whom you don't have any feelings at all, a near stranger. But you could imagine, perhaps, meeting that person at work or on the street and exchanging an honest, friendly greeting, full of goodwill, and see what feelings follow that thought. Or you might imagine other people in that person's life who really care for him a lot, and gently turn over words like "May he be happy!" in your mind.

Perhaps you've guessed the next stage. Yes: it's someone whom you just don't like. Spurred on by the positive feelings and goodwill that arose more easily in the earlier stages of the practice, the challenge is to wish happiness to this difficult, irritating individual for whom you do not normally feel anything approaching goodwill. And the meditation practice can go on to take us as far as we like: including more and more people in our well-wishing. We might include other people in the building we're in, in the street outside, across the city, in countries with which we're at war. We could take our goodwill to more friends, our friends' friends, those whom they know in their own turn and on to the ends of the world. As one of the earliest Buddhist scriptures puts it:

> . . . *Even as a mother protects with her life*
> *Her child, her only child,*
> *So with a boundless heart*
> *Should one cherish all living beings;*
> *Radiating kindness over the entire world:*
> *Spreading upwards to the skies,*
> *And downwards to the depths;*
> *Outwards and unbounded . . .*[11]

Doing a practice like this regularly has profound consequences. Traditionally, it has been said to promote good health (conversely, chronic ill will and stress-related illness often go hand in hand). Buddhaghosa, an ancient Buddhist commentator, even said that regular practice of the Development of Loving-Kindness would lead to good looks, as the furrows of persistent annoyance leave the brow. At our core it is creating a powerful inclination to act kindly wherever we have the opportunity. That entails coming into imaginative relationship with others, rather than seeing them as separate, unrelated adversaries. To do this requires training.

Why not start now?

## TRY THIS: THE MEDITATION ON LOVING-KINDNESS
This is one of several traditional Buddhist meditation practices that are designed to help us deal with our emotions. If you can do it regularly, even after a few days you will start to find that it changes the overall emotional tone of your daily life. Over time, it can help to replace your feelings of irritation with those of goodwill.

The practice is divided into five stages of more or less equal length. To start with, you could devote just a few minutes—no more than five—to each stage. Later on, with more practice, you can gradually extend the meditation to ten or even more minutes per stage.

---

11. Karaniya Metta Sutta, *Sutta Nipata* 1.8.

Meditation is not meant to be any kind of endurance test: like anything, the better we prepare the better the results. So before you start meditating, spend a little time to get ready for the practice.

Preparation: Pick a place where you can be undisturbed, and wear loose-fitting clothes. You'll want to find a way of sitting still that's most natural for you, in which you can be both comfortable and alert. You may have seen pictures of people meditating in the lotus position: that's great if you can do it comfortably, but it's certainly not essential. You could try kneeling with your buttocks supported on a stack of cushions and your knees on the floor, or you can meditate just as well sitting in a chair. We'd suggest a hard-backed chair, because that helps you sit upright. Let your feet rest on the floor, and your hands rest on your lap to take any strain off the shoulders. And then we let ourselves relax. One way of doing this is to become aware of the body: perhaps beginning with the feet, feeling their contact with the floor, feeling the weight of the legs, the chair beneath us and so on, slowly scanning upward. We can feel the rise and fall of the chest and belly as we breathe, feel the balance of the head on the shoulders. When you're ready, let your eyes close and start the first stage of the practice.

Stage One. In the first stage you try to cultivate feelings of loving-kindness toward yourself. One way of doing this is to recite over and over to yourself, in your mind: "May I be well, may I be happy, may I progress." And why not? Why shouldn't you be well and happy and make spiritual progress? In fact, why shouldn't everyone enjoy these great benefits? That is what this meditation is all about. We all need to find for ourselves the most natural way to wish ourselves well. Try these ideas and see what works best for you:

- ▾ Imagine yourself surrounded by light of a beautiful color
- ▾ Imagine yourself in a particularly beautiful place
- ▾ Recall a time when you were particularly happy
- ▾ Bring to mind something that you did that you can be proud of

You may well find that this leaves you feeling really good. That's great, but remember the real point of the practice is not the good feelings that you are experiencing: it's the fact that you are wishing them on yourself, and then going on to wish happiness on others.

Stage Two. In the second stage, you call to mind a friend. Try to imagine your friend as vividly as you can. We recommend choosing someone who is not a sexual partner, but who is of a similar age to yourself (for otherwise your feelings of loving-kindness may be confused with parental, filial or sexual impulses). Bearing your friend in mind, try to develop strong feelings of loving-kindness toward that person. Again, you can recite to yourself, in your mind, "May my friend be well, be happy, make progress." Or you might try some of the ideas that worked well for you: perhaps imagining your friend surrounded by a beautiful light. Try to be aware of the actual feelings that you experience as you keep your friend in mind in these ways. Where you feel warmth, or currents of goodwill, acknowledge them and you'll find that they start to grow.

Stage Three. In the third stage, let your mind dwell on a "neutral" person. This might be someone at work with whom you have fairly regular contact, but for whom you don't feel any strong feelings one way or the other. It might be someone you see regularly when you shop, for example. Again, you try to experience a sense of loving-kindness toward her. "May she be well, may she be happy, may she progress." Any of the ideas that helped you develop kindness toward yourself or your friend will work with the "neutral" person also.

Stage Four. Here, we call to mind someone we find difficult. To begin with, it's best not to focus on a sworn enemy. Try someone with whom your communication is a little abrasive, perhaps a friend with whom communication has broken down, and try to develop feelings of loving-kindness toward him. "May he be well, may he be happy, may he make progress."

Stage Five. In the fifth and final stage you bring to mind all four people: yourself, your friend, the "neutral" person and the enemy.

Imagine all of you together in the same space. Here, we try to feel feelings of warmth and loving-kindness for all four, equally, using words or images to help us. From there, you begin to radiate that feeling of loving-kindness outward. Begin with everyone in your immediate locale, then reach out into the neighborhood, the town, the county, the country, the continent, the world—ultimately radiating feelings of warmth and loving-kindness to all living beings everywhere.

The loving-kindness meditation is a powerfully transforming practice. Once they have a little experience of it, most people find that they can use it almost without fail to bring about an improvement in their current mental state. If you practice it regularly over a sufficient period of time, you'll come to develop reserves of loving-kindness that you can call upon more or less at will.

## Transforming the World Through Work

The world of work provides us with many opportunities to act kindly. It may seem that teachers, health-care workers, and people working in the overseas aid sector are at an advantage when it comes to acting kindly in their work. Many people will understandably want to take a much more radical approach to helping the suffering than even the idea of "kindness" suggests. If we look around and open our eyes to the suffering that surrounds us, we see what seems to be a growing, excluded underclass in the developed world and extraordinary poverty and suffering in the undeveloped world. In the face of this, some will regard it as absurd to devote time to things like meditation and the refining of an ethical practice. As people of good faith they'll just want to get out there and do something to help relieve the suffering they encounter. But the Buddhist way is to look before we leap.

It's true that all of us, in our own ways—even radical ways—can probably do much more to improve the lot of others. If we don't make a career of it we might volunteer our spare time. That is generally to the good. But none of this should exclude our attempts to develop kindness. If we really want to help others, really want to change the world for the better, we'll need to grow kinder too.

Viradhamma, who lives with his wife and son in Berkeley, California, teaches at the San Francisco Buddhist Center and is devoted to meditation, study and the practice of the Buddhist precepts. He works in the finance department of a city government where he is responsible for the municipal budget of $180 million. He prepares the long-range budget forecasts for the city and negotiates labor agreements and contracts with private companies to run city functions.

The way he earns his living today is, in many ways, a far cry from a task he did many years ago as the program director for a non-profit organization that sent volunteers from the United States and Europe to aid various ministries and organizations in Nicaragua during the Sandinista's period of government. Not surprisingly, the people who were drawn to work in that organization were all very idealistic. They certainly weren't in it for the money. Viradhamma met many wonderful people, several of whom became close friends.

> People felt they were dealing with things that were very immediate, and in fact some people we were working with were being shot at and some of them were getting killed. It was a very poignant and emotionally charged environment to work in. But the thing that struck me after having worked there for three or four years was that, although everybody had a very clear sense of common purpose, people had a hard time getting along.
>
> Untold hours were wasted solving problems which objectively looked like they weren't very big at all. One of my jobs was to help screen volunteers who were going to

Nicaragua, to find out why they were going and what their actual motivation was. I mean what their real motivation was, beneath what they said, sometimes even beneath what they felt. It became clear to me after a few years that the people working there, as well as those volunteering, brought tremendous creativity and energy and idealism to the task. But a lot of them had this two or three percent problem in terms of how they got along with people. Or some had bad habits when it came to dealing with others. Or there were certain areas where they didn't know themselves and so acted irrationally. They all had a lot to give, but with so many of them there was this tiny character flaw, and we seemed to spend forty to fifty percent of our time as a group trying to sort out those flaws.

I know it's a kind of simplistic question that a lot of social activists have put to themselves over the years, but I had to ask "Do you reform society first and then go to work on the people or do you reform the people first and then go to work on society?" I'd come to the organization feeling pretty strongly that there's a big case to be made for first reforming society and then letting the people sort themselves out afterwards. But I went through a change while I was working there because I began to see very clearly that if we could just deal with those one or two or three percent personal problems, and the low-level unskillful behavior that people were bringing to the work, then the amount of energy to transform society that would be liberated would be astonishing.

I'd had some contact with Buddhism before, but now I decided to take it more seriously. I started meditating because I knew that I had my own character flaws and I saw I could change those by practicing Buddhism and through meditation and reflection.

When I left that arena of work I decided that I had a real interest in making a commitment to Buddhism, to using it as a

means of social transformation. Teaching at the Buddhist
center, leading retreats, these are now my main practices, the
way I try to effect positive change in the world. The Buddha's
teachings can transform societies, they can transform
workplaces and communities.

We could think of others we know personally who might also be
changing the world for the better in ways that aren't obvious. There
is George, who works for a major automobile manufacturer as part
of a team that is trying to design the first commercially viable elec-
trically powered automobile. Think about the positive impact of his
work on the environment. Then there is Angela, who works for a
major supermarket chain and helped to re-design their checkout
system so as to make the work of the checkout clerks both more efficient and more humane.

The way we change the world may have little to do with our job
description. Pauline works in the mailroom of a large corporation,
playing her part in getting everyone's mail to them efficiently.
Everyone in her department relies on her as someone they can
really talk to when times are tough. She is always there, willing to
listen, openhearted and generous with her time and attention. In
another setting, the best salespeople will at times tell their customers not to buy what's on sale, because they have enough empathetic understanding to see that their customer doesn't really need
it. And, in the same way that the meditation practice we described
above might help your looks, those salespeople will be the ones
who find their customers coming back again and again. The really
good business consultants don't just solve problems: they care
imaginatively about their clients and try to help them succeed. If
we want to know the net effect of our job on the world, we need
to go beyond the obvious. But one thing is sure. Regular practice of
the loving-kindness meditation *will* have a positive effect on your
working life.

Take Ed Piercy for example. Ed is the deputy principal of a high school in Cambridge, England, where he teaches economics and business studies. He makes a point of teaching these subjects in a way that stresses the human dimension of economic experience.

"People are more than just economic agents and I think it's important to present the material in ways that cause my students to consider the ethical issues that emerge from economic and business policy decisions. The classical economic model that the syllabus requires me to teach, for example, assumes that the desirable goal of low inflation can only be achieved at the cost of unemployment. I teach that, but in the process I try to make my students aware of what unemployment actually means to people and I ask them to consider the value of a policy, the achievement of which involves human suffering. Whether or not the relationship between inflation and unemployment is inescapably the case, what matters most to me is that my students consider the human dimension of such issues."

The same applies in business studies, where Ed tries to get his students to think deeply about how the different business models they look at impact upon the lives of employees, customers and the environment. "The syllabus effectively requires only knowledge and analysis of theories and models. But I feel I can't leave it there. I'm not just teaching students to pass exams, I'm trying to teach them to be responsible adults in a difficult modern society."

Ed's practice of the meditation on loving-kindness has led him to a greater awareness of his responsibility to himself and to others. "I've come to see that everyone has the same goal as I have—everyone wants to be happy—and we all experience similar difficulties in pursuit of that goal. That realization has really helped me in my dealings with difficult students and colleagues."

For Ed, the third, fourth and much of the fifth stages of the practice—the neutral person, the enemy and the wider world—are occupied by people from his school, and practicing in that way has significantly transformed his relations there. "The people I've put in those stages have, over time, all become real human beings for me—they've all got their own lives, their own difficulties, but we all share the desire to be happy."

Since taking up the loving-kindness meditation practice, Ed has noticed that his relationships with the people he works with have significantly changed. "When I started doing the practice I was teaching a class of rowdy teenagers, and I put several of them in the fourth stage. I was astonished to discover how after doing that, even the next day, my relationship to them noticeably improved, and that had an effect on the whole class. Because I'd changed in how I related to them, they changed in relation to me."

Valerie Kenyon attributes the promotion she received at work directly to her practice of the loving-kindness meditation. She is a senior manager, responsible for quality and technical matters, at a confectionery factory in Croydon, just south of London, and she learned the practice at the Croydon Buddhist Centre.

"Previously I'd been the laboratory manager, and that was a responsible position, but I only had four other people working under me and that suited me then. I was very shy and introverted, not at all confident around other people. I used to be terrified if I ever had to go out to visit suppliers or attend conferences."

Three or four years after taking up the meditation on loving-kindness, however, all of that began noticeably to change.

"It took a while to show, but gradually my attitudes to other people started to change in significant ways. When I got the promotion, my boss told me that I'd been given it because they'd noticed how much I'd changed. I'd grown friendlier and more confident, and they liked my style of working."

Now Valerie is in charge of quality and technical matters throughout the factory, working with the various production managers, telling them what they have to do to improve and maintain quality—effectively overseeing the work of 250 people. She could never have done that earlier. She just didn't have the confidence.

She has enjoyed her work much more since the promotion. Previously she was planning to leave, but since moving up she has found the job pleasingly challenging. She's glad to be earning an appreciably higher salary, of course, but she especially enjoys the human side of things, which previously she found so difficult.

"I got the job because they saw that I don't go around with the attitude 'Oh I'm the manager and you've got to do what I say!' Instead, I try to take people individually into account and see what their actual needs are. I make a point of approaching issues in the spirit of friendliness, and that's then reflected back at me. People respond so much better when you approach them with kindness. It's obvious, of course, but not everyone does it."

One of the coordinators Valerie works with had a big difficulty with one of her own subordinates. She would get terribly frustrated and angry with her. But her coordinator knows a little about what Valerie does in meditation, and one day they discussed the difficulty she was having with her subordinate.

"You just shouldn't let it get to you like that," Valerie told her. "It's not good for you and it's not good for the other person either. Instead, try to understand her, try to see what's going on. And try to think of her with thoughts of loving-kindness." And Valerie explained a little about the practice to her.

"Now, whenever she sees me, and she's a bit het up, she says 'I know, I know—loving-kindness . . .' And it's a bit of a joke between us, but I can see that it's really had a good effect and she's starting to make some progress with it."

Valerie has also found that by approaching people in the spirit of loving-kindness she can help to spread a more ethical approach to the work amongst her colleagues.

"It's really easy there to pilfer a box of chocolates, or to use the office photocopier for personal copying. But I just tell people 'That's stealing, you know.' Because I do it in a straightforward, lighthearted way, they don't take offense and the message gets across. I also notice that gossiping and the use of foul language don't go on around me, which is quite unusual in a British factory. People know I don't like it and they don't do it."

## Assessing Ourselves in the World of Work

How might we assess our work and its consequences? We recommend following the same progression that we saw in the Development of Loving-Kindness meditation. We need to avoid grandiose abstraction, and a good way to do so is to start close to home, with ourselves, looking at the impact of our job on our own lives, in terms of the balance of harm and goodness. Then we could go on to consider what it does to those we most care about, such as our families and close friends, and then consider its impact on those we care little for, or even dislike. Finally, we can ask ourselves what it does to the world. We asked Jerry Freeman to perform this five-stage self-assessment and he was surprised at what he learned.

Jerry had a senior position in a major international mining company. At the time, he was becoming a more and more serious Buddhist practitioner, and was trying to gain some clarity about how his work was affecting the world and whether he needed to change what he was doing. We'll cover quite a lot of what Jerry had to say, because his experience of self-assessment can provide useful hints to any of us, even if our own jobs are very different.

Here's what Jerry found as he started with himself and then worked outward.

"That job gave me my first taste of taking on responsibility in the real world," he said. Previously, working as a geologist, he'd done quite rarefied jobs with very talented and capable people who were all like him in terms of age, career development and training. Now, as a manager, he had to learn to relate to a much wider range of people, from all walks of life. That enriched him as a person and it helped him to mature. "I'd been the bright kid flying in and out with mineral samples. But now I had to stand my ground and be more adult."

Another really important benefit that Jerry found in this job was his boss, Pierre. "This was someone with very little formal education who'd joined the organization at the age of sixteen as an apprentice lab assistant on one of the mines." Pierre had worked his way up to the top of the company over four decades and was a role model to Jerry as he'd been for many other younger managers over the years. "What struck me about Pierre was the way he took a stand on the things that mattered to him with complete transparency and consistency. I often disagreed him, but I knew I could rely on him." Jerry valued the fatherly interest his boss took in him. "The lasting benefit I took from my time with Pierre was that through him I learned about being a mentor to others."

The job also gave him a welcome sense of security. "The early 1990s were very difficult times in an industry like mine, but it didn't seem to worry me too much. Even if my position went, as I thought it might well do at the bottom of the recession, I knew that I'd get plenty of warning and every help in approaching headhunters in the right way to get a similar job elsewhere."

Jerry went on to consider how his job helped those close to him. "I found it much easier to spend time with my girlfriend. I'd had very little control over where I'd be at any time in my previous job, and that had been starting to destroy our relationship. Then my father got cancer. I was the only child and it would have been so hard on him if I'd been stuck with the travel schedule that I used to have. I just couldn't have given him the support he needed." The job was quite well paid too, so Jerry could help his mother when times got harder for her when Jerry's dad died, buying her a new car and contributing to the cost of her home.

"I wouldn't say that any of the people working with me there became close friends," said Jerry. "But a lot of good things were happening, as I look back on it all." Julie, one of Jerry's subordinates, was a seemingly tough accountant who talked little about her personal life. As Julie started taking a series of uncharacteristic absences from work, it emerged that she was having a difficult time with her long-term boyfriend. Jerry arranged for her to have paid leave and persuaded the company to provide counseling and mediation services: all of this was ordinarily available only to married employees. That made a big difference to her life.

Karl worked in Jerry's department, on loan to the company's head office from its German subsidiary. "It was the recession," said Jerry. "Karl wasn't right for the job and we had to reduce staff anyway. Karl was going to lose his job. He had two kids at a critical stage in a local high school. They'd been through all the disruption of relocating into a different language environment. It was going to be really hard on that family if they were sent back home so soon. Karl and I managed to work out some genuinely useful projects outside his job description that kept things going for the extra year he needed. But then there was the contract nightmare."

The company's lawyers took the view that Karl's transfer had voided his original German contract, and that Karl had no right to severance pay. "It seemed like this was going on for weeks and weeks between me, the lawyers, Karl and the HR department," said Jerry. "Finally I'd had enough." Jerry wrote an official letter on company stationery, in his capacity as Karl's line manager, saying that the company would honor all of Karl's original contractual rights, including his layoff entitlements. "Human Resources went ballistic! A really nasty memo got sent up to my boss Pierre more or less calling for my head on a plate." Jerry was told that he'd stepped way out of line. "But Pierre also told me that he'd have done just the same in my situation. Nothing bad happened to me in consequence. It taught me that I had quite a lot of power to do good, or at least to prevent harm, much more than I'd thought possible."

Bill worked for Jerry in a junior role. He'd been a teacher, hated it, had drifted into the company in a clerical position and, although capable, seemed lacking in direction. Jerry trained him and moved him up through his department until he thought Bill was ready to study part-time for an MBA. Since then, Bill's career has taken off and he's in a senior finance role elsewhere in the company.

"As I did my self-assessment," he continued, "I was struck by just how many opportunities there had been to make the jobs of those working with me and for me more creative and interesting." Jerry was able to help some of them to play a larger role within the company, or develop potential that had not before been recognized. There was more. Before Jerry came along the company was making bad investment decisions to the point where it was under the threat of takeover. Jerry figured that his work helped to change that, saving people's jobs and leaving the company better placed to cope with the recession. "When I was a technical specialist, ordinary people had been numbers. Now they had faces and that meant that good investment decisions really mattered, because they helped real people."

How did his work allow him to act kindly to those he disliked? It became apparent to him that senior managers in some parts of the company were secretly setting prices for contracts with their competitors. "That made me really angry when I got to know what they were up to," Jerry said. "Here were these losers putting so much at risk for everyone. The competition regulators would have shown us no mercy had there been an investigation." But Jerry helped them to find legitimate alternatives to that way of doing things, initially by starting a discussion about the practice that others had been unwilling to look at. We asked him if he'd ever considered reporting the matter to the authorities. "No point," he said. "All that happens is that someone lower down the food chain would be made to take the fall and then the pattern would be repeated." Instead, he decided to try to change the pattern. And he'd been able to do it in a way that was kind, creative and effective toward people he found really difficult.

Finally, Jerry wondered how his job was making the world a better place. The extraction of industrial minerals didn't seem to have much to do directly with world salvation.

"What I did is not very dramatic. In fact it's really ordinary: countless people are doing the kinds of good things that this self-assessment shows I did."

Nonetheless, Jerry had been surprised to find how much his

self-assessment revealed that was worthwhile. And he found the ordinariness of it strangely inspiring.

"It makes me kind of confident and optimistic to know that you don't have to be a saint, that anyone can make a difference in these kinds of ways."

Unspectacular acts of kindness in the workplace can transform the world, like ripples spreading from a pebble thrown into a lake, as others start to get the idea also. Any of us can practice kindness in our work, and a self-assessment of what we're already doing will probably surprise us and give us the confidence to do more and more.

Here's how Jerry's reflections would look if set out on the kind of simple assessment form that anyone can use.

Benefits to self

*Taste of real world. Grew up somewhat*

*Boss as good role model*

*Job security*

Benefits to those close to him

*More time with partner*

*More time with dad*

*Financial help for mom*

Benefits to neutral people

*Made job more creative for some people*

*Helped Julie with counseling*

*Helped Karl over severance issue*

*Helped Bill with MBA*

*Helped improve investment decisions*

Benefits to difficult people

*Stopped cartel*

Benefits to the world

*Cascade of ordinary kindness*

But for Jerry, his job wasn't all positive, any more than it would be for any of us.

Jerry came to the job from a very professional, technical, meritocratic background in which office politics had not been tolerated. Initially, he found the amount of politics that he encountered in the mining company bizarre, and then he found it tiresome as he had to involve himself in the politics more and more. Then it became deeply upsetting. When some of those he'd defended turned their knives on him, he had a deep sense of betrayal, unfairness and helplessness. This seemed all the more unpleasant when he contrasted it with the behavior he encountered amongst the Buddhist friends he was making at the time, or when he contrasted his feelings at the end of a fraught meeting with the mental states he was hoping to develop through meditation.

Then there was the question of his values. Jerry believes that businesses should promote diversity, and the company had adopted a model policy on HIV and AIDS that he drew to friends' attention with some pride. But he found it painful to listen to the homophobic jokes being told in the executive suite when the policy was being discussed. His boss Pierre once asked him about another senior manager who was being considered for promotion to look after overseas interests. "I need to know whether he's fit to represent us. We've got to bear in mind that he'll be meeting heads of state. Do you reckon he's a fag?" Jerry made a dismissive comment claiming ignorance, and the conversation moved on. But he could not help but feel dismay at both the question and his own response.

Jerry himself came up for promotion after a while and the company wanted him to run a significant operation in the developing world. That would have meant schmoozing with politicians, and being responsible for the payment of what were described as commissions to agents working with government officials. Lars, who'd been doing that job previously and was about to retire, told him something of what would be involved. "And if you're lucky, you might make a buck or two." Jerry chose not to probe what Lars was driving at, but it sounded suspiciously like taking a cut of some bribes.

Increasingly, Jerry found that, for all the good things that the job did for him, it was starting to take a toll on his own well-being. It was also having negative effects on those close to him.

"I used to bitch and moan about all of this to my partner, more or less every evening. She's a great woman, but, boy, it must have been tedious for her to listen to. She had her own job to do as well. It was like that old Californian joke: I've said enough about me—now let's hear what you've got to say about me."

There were so many other, much richer things to talk about, like their growing involvement in Buddhism, which never really got enough attention. People farther from home were affected too.

"Looking back, I'm sure the company panicked when the recession came. We closed three mines in one of our major regions. We could have got away with shutting one, especially as demand swung back much faster than we'd expected. A lot of jobs were lost unnecessarily, and with those losses went a lot of suffering." It's always seductive to try to put the world right with hindsight, but Jerry thinks that he could have made much more use of his influence to prevent that kind of panicked response. He also played a large part in enabling acquisitions of other businesses that powerful board members were pushing through for little more reason than self-importance. "I tried not to think about it too much, but then the financial press got hold of it and I felt like such a fool. I could have spoken my mind. And bad decisions like that put lots of people's jobs at risk."

"I never had the chance to have a go at my enemies. But by the end I really wanted to. I can remember a Buddhist meditation retreat when all sorts of intriguing ideas for vengeance would pop into my mind whenever I was supposed to be doing that meditation on Loving-Kindness. . . ."

The company was one of the better operators in its sector. But this was a part of the industry where it was notoriously difficult to keep clean hands. "You can stay squeaky-clean if you like. But you'll have to pull the business out of here," one country manager told Jerry. "Then you'll feel good and none of the rest of us will be able to make any more contributions to those who have to live here." Jerry could see the point, but nonetheless felt that there was a lot of special pleading and that his company could have been more scrupulous in some of its dealings.

And there was the question of environmental damage. On one overseas visit Jerry was touring the jungles in a mountainous area where the rock pinnacles are outstandingly beautiful, swirling with mist in the river gorges. But the pinnacles were also mineral rich. "Right, guys," said the mining engineer he was with. "We'll blast that face there and take those ones down from the top. . . . Pretty, aren't they?" he observed to Jerry. "Still, you can't eat the view." Jerry said nothing.

"There I was," Jerry told us, "in a really senior position, but not doing what I really wanted in the world given the situation and my place in it."

Here's the other side of Jerry's self-assessment. It shows the harm that his job does to himself, his friends and family, and it expands out to include those less close to him and ultimately takes in the world.

Negative effects on self
>  *Playing at company politics*
>  *Betraying some of his principles*
>  *Involvement in dirty world—bribes, etc.*

Negative effects on those close to him
>  *Boring his partner*
>  *Personal unhappiness from work affected others outside work*

Negative effects on neutral people

*Closed too many factories*

*Bad acquisitions*

Negative effects on difficult people

*None: for want of opportunity!*

Negative effects on the world

*Ethical issues in developing world*

*Environmental degradation*

While Jerry was up for promotion, another opportunity, outside the company, came up which promised far fewer negative factors. His boss told him that he'd respect whatever Jerry finally decided. Jerry quit. "We value you and want to keep you, but I'm not at all surprised," said Pierre, his boss. "It was getting obvious that you weren't happy here. The promotion offer means you know you had a choice. You've decided for yourself just what you want to do." Today, Jerry has no regrets whatsoever about his time in the mining company. "It was right to move on, it wasn't the right place for me anymore, but doing the self-assessment made me feel curiously grateful. I learned to make more and more grown-up choices in that messy, human world." In the end, Jerry moved on not so much because he found the mining job ethically difficult, but because he was becoming more and more clear about what mattered to him. "The difficulties were more to do with me than with them: of not making more use of the personal power that I really had all along." The appeal of his next job was that it gave him so many more opportunities to express what he cared about. He's also earning significantly more money, which is not coincidental: it's become easier for him to focus his energies and do his job even better than before.

A famous psychologist, Abraham Maslow, wrote about what people look for in their jobs. He uncovered a hierarchy of needs. At the bottom of the hierarchy, people go to work because they need some money: to pay for food and shelter. But once that need is satisfied, we want something more. Beyond food and shelter, Maslow said, we go to work for the possibilities of human communication. Beyond that, we look for identity. When people say "Tell me about yourself," so often we start to describe our jobs. At the top of Maslow's hierarchy is what he calls "self-actualization": our job is a stage on which we can act out the meaning of many aspects of our lives. And that meaning is to be found in the way in which we, like Jerry, grapple with the question of how we make a difference, for good or ill, to ourselves, others and the world.

Perhaps no job is perfectly skillful. In the end, we have to make an imperfect judgment. The question is, are we doing that with awareness and honesty, and in the light of a set of viable ethical precepts? Take some time to make an assessment of your own job. When you've set it all down, how, on balance, do you feel about it? Jerry felt he had to move on from his job. Could you change yours for the better? What positive aspects of it can you strengthen? Which negative aspects can you reduce?

TRY THIS: ASSESSING YOUR WORK
You might complete this assessment by yourself, or find a trusted colleague, friend or partner to work through it with you.

Benefits to yourself

Benefits to those close to you

Benefits to neutral people

Benefits to difficult people

Benefits to the world

Negative effects on yourself

Negative effects on those close to you

Negative effects on neutral people

Negative effects on difficult people

Negative effects on the world

-----------------------------------------------------------------

-----------------------------------------------------------------

-----------------------------------------------------------------

When you've done your assessment, reflect on your job. How, on balance, do you feel about it?

- How has the balance of positive and negative been changing over time?
- Are there things you can change for the better?
- What positive aspects of it can you strengthen?
- Which negative aspects can you reduce?

Make an action plan based on these questions, then set yourself a time frame for implementing any changes.

# FIVE

# The Second Precept: Develop Generosity

*Don't take what hasn't been freely given to you,
instead develop generosity.*

When we take from others against their will we strengthen the barrier between self and the world and increase our experience of isolation. Few readers of this book will be hardened criminals, but it's worth reflecting for a moment or two on other areas of taking which may elude us—all those petty "victimless crimes" that are so easy to overlook. Need a few envelopes at home? Well, slip a few into your bag from the stationery cupboard at work. No one will mind (and no one will notice). Or, "I wonder how much that shirt cost, the one that got lost with my luggage? Was it thirty dollars? Oh, call it fifty. . . ." It's easy to fudge items on our insurance claims, tax returns and expense forms.

But there *are* no victimless crimes, someone always has to pay for what we consume. Not only that—we ourselves become the victims of our own vagueness and self-concern when we act in this way. It perpetuates our habits of self-preoccupation and unawareness and so we live less fully and less happily than we might otherwise.

Nor do we only take financially. We can also take other people's time and energy. You know that person at work, the one whom everyone will do almost anything to avoid? When you fall into his clutches he keeps talking on and on and on, regardless of what you were on your way to do when he pounced—and regardless of whether you're actually listening. And there are the emotional vampires, people who are always having such a dreadful time (or so they think) and who really need a shoulder to cry on—again.

All these ways of taking what isn't freely given work against our own best interests in the long run. If I take from you in this way, I am polarizing our relationship. I am reinforcing a view that you are an alien entity whom I don't need to take into consideration. That behavior underscores our sense of separateness from others, and makes us, in the end, unhappier than we might otherwise be. So, if we want to move toward Enlightenment, it is important to work at reducing the amount we take that is not freely given. It isn't very hard to be that little bit more ethically scrupulous, and that will help us to be free from remorse and therefore happier. But if we want to really transform ourselves in this area, we can go still further. We can develop generosity, which will bring us the gift of ever greater abundance in our lives.

## What the Buddha Taught About Generosity

The Buddha encouraged everyone to give, no matter how small their means. "If you have little, give a little," he said. "If you have a medium amount, give a medium amount. If you have a lot, give a lot. . . . Share your wealth. Use it. Follow the noble path. If you eat alone, you won't eat happily."[12]

Once, he was talking to a large crowd of monks and nuns, about five hundred of them, and they were all set to get the very

---

12. Jataka V. 382.

latest spiritual teaching—direct from the master himself. They were so eager to hear the Buddha's latest thoughts that nobody noticed, right there in the middle of the gathering, a person who hadn't eaten for days. They got a teaching—but it was not one that they had expected. The Buddha refused to say a word until that person had been fed.[13] "If people knew as I know the benefits of giving and sharing," he said on another occasion, "they would not use things without sharing them. Stinginess would never find a place in their hearts. Even down to their last morsel of food, they would not use it without sharing if there were anyone else to share it with."[14]

Some people are generous by nature. The rest of us have to work at it. Buddhism has always regarded generosity as something that needs to be cultivated and, like all things that we have to learn, the more we practice it the better we become. Starting with small things, we can build up from there, giving more and more until in time we come to develop a completely free, totally generous nature.

Generosity has always been the pre-eminent Buddhist virtue. Buddhist scriptures are full of it. Perhaps you've got friends who've visited a Buddhist temple in one of the Eastern countries. The tourists tend to pass through by day. But if you were there in the evening or on a full-moon day, you could sit with the local people swapping gossip and listening to the monk or lama—often on a high throne surrounded by garlands of flowers—giving them a reminder about the Buddhist way of life. Nine times out of ten you'll find that he's speaking about generosity.

Why should it be so important? In the first place, it goes right to the heart of the problem of suffering, of living a life that falls short of our potential. That's the problem of seeing ourselves as separate from everyone and everything else, of seeing ourselves as the center of the whole world. By giving, we break down the walls

13. Dhammapada Commentary, book 15, story 5.
14. Ittivutaka 26.

that divide us from the rest of the world, and we start to get a taste of what it might be like to experience the open dimension of life, when we don't live life just in terms of "me" and "mine." Giving is the opposite of grasping. It's a way in which we can directly reverse the harmful tendency that we saw at work earlier in this book, when we described the Wheel of Money: the self-referential tendency that throttles our existence. Giving is an indispensable aspect of the Path of Abundance.

Giving also tops the list of virtues for a very practical reason. It's something that anyone can do. We might not be particularly "moral" in a conventional religious sense. We might be partial to a drink too many, or have a bit too much of a roving eye. We might find meditation really difficult: we might squirm in distracted discomfort after just five minutes on our chair or meditation mat. We may prefer airport thrillers and pulp romances to the wisdom of the ages. We may not think that we're all that spiritual. But at least we can give. However bad you may think you are, you can, right here and now, give something to someone and rekindle your own hope and confidence.

When we are generous, we experience ourselves differently: if you're not happy with yourself, try giving, and see what happens. The idea that giving makes us happier and that it can also mitigate the effects of past unskillful acts is very familiar to those who have been brought up in traditional Buddhist cultures.

## Giving as an Antidote to Unskillfulness

Jayasiri is a Sri Lankan student of Kulananda's, whose upbringing led him to view things somewhat differently from Kulananda's Western students. One day, he was having a bad time with stomach pain and Kulananda was concerned. His first thought was that if the Pepto-Bismol wasn't working, Jayasiri needed to get down to the doctor's office. Jayasiri disagreed. He'd done something that he believed was unskillful the day before. It was preying on his mind and that, he told Kulananda, was why he was hurting.

Kulananda responded as he would have done to any of his Western students. "Let's talk about what you did," he said. "Yes, it was unskillful, but was it really so bad? We all do unskillful things from time to time. . . ."

"Look, this isn't helping," Jayasiri said. "I don't need you to let me off the hook." And Kulananda wasn't sure where to take the conversation next.

The next day, a Saturday, when they met in the evening, Jayasiri told Kulananda that his stomach pains had gone. "Did you go and see a doctor?" Kulananda asked. "No need," said Jayasiri, and he told Kulananda what he'd done.

He decided he needed to create some positive karma for himself. From time to time he volunteered at a local retirement home, so he'd called the supervisor and booked himself in for an extra shift, spending the day talking with some of the lonelier people there. He felt a lot better about himself from doing that and that translated into feeling physically better. By giving, he had turned himself around. Giving is something we can always do to get the wind back in our sails, to recover the initiative in our lives.

Giving provides a point of purchase on the rock face of the spiritual life, indeed, of life itself. And conversely, someone who is not generous, who doesn't give, will find the spiritual life quite out of reach. If you can't give, then you won't live much of a life at all. From a Buddhist standpoint it's not enough to be well versed in Buddhist scripture and philosophy. You might live strictly by the traditional precepts, avoiding all forbidden activities: taking life, theft, sexual misconduct, dishonesty and intoxication, but that's not enough. There are those who call themselves Buddhists who eat no meat, steal no office stationery, have no sex, tell no lies and blanch at a beer, but until they start giving—something, anything—there is no hope for them.

## Giving in Traditional Buddhism

In the Buddha's day, his monastic disciples depended, as he himself did, on alms: that is, on whatever food they could collect in their alms bowls on their daily round when householders who wanted to support the monastic community would make offerings of food. In some Buddhist countries, this practice of begging has continued right up to the present day. It has even come to the West. Traditionally, it is said, the point of this practice wasn't just to ensure a free meal for the monks and nuns. It was also, and crucially, to provide ordinary people with a chance to give, to get their first toehold on the difficult ascent of the path of generosity.

When his first Western monastic disciples returned home, Ajahn Chah, a Thai teacher and one of the founders of the Forest tradition of Buddhism, insisted that they keep up their alms round when they came to the West—going out in the early morning through the streets of London, making themselves available for offerings from those who wanted to support them. Monks and nuns don't "beg" in the common use of that word. Their rule forbids them from asking for anything. They stand and wait, eyes cast down, their bowls half-concealed under their robes. Those who want to give, do; those who'd rather ignore them, can.

Ajahn Chah's reasons for insisting on the alms round were not primarily economic. "First of all you are going to be strange there," he said, "wearing robes and with shaved heads, and people don't like to feel strange, so if there's nothing to get you outside of the monastery you're going to stay in there all the time—and you're going to end up driving each other crazy and arguing all the time. But secondly, it's your duty as a monk to wave the Buddha's flag. It doesn't matter if people don't understand Buddhism or what you are, if they just see someone who is peaceful and composed, walking down the street, then that's a message to them."

"But they don't know about the alms round in the West," his disciples objected. "No one's going to give us any food."

"Do you mean to say there are no kind people in the West?" Ajahn Chah asked.

When a monastery in Mendocino County was established, in the Ajahn Chah tradition, its leader, Ajahn Amaro decided it was time to take up the practice of going on an alms round in Ukiah, a small town nearby.

"We just went one day, we walked through the town and came back, and the first time we didn't get anything. But it's such a small town that word of what we were doing soon spread. Now we go every week and we get more food than we can eat.

"A little while ago some of us were walking past this garage with our alms bowls and this guy came out, a mechanic who'd just been underneath a car and was covered in grease, and he said, 'Oh, can you guys eat chocolate cake?' And we said, 'Yes.' So he rushed off into the back room, got this plate full of chocolate cake, and then stood there, looking at his greasy hands and looking at the cake. . . . Because we can't reach over and take things, they have to be put in our bowls. So eventually he got the paper plate and just tipped it into my bowl. Wonderful! He was just a regular local guy."

Amaro is concerned that the economic imperatives under which some lay Western Buddhist teachers labor may have the effect of distorting their teaching.

"I think that it's generally a grave mistake for someone to be a professional Buddhist teacher. Because most of the lay teachers are family people and to pay the mortgage and be able to send their kids to college, they've got to keep the money rolling in. And I don't know any Buddhist teachers who are prepared to live in a trailer park. Most of them live very much an upper-middle-class lifestyle and there's a constant temptation, based on economic pressures, to please everyone and be all things to all people. But the job of a Buddhist teacher is to point out the way for people to go against the stream of self-centered craving. To do that you have to challenge them. And if you sculpt the teaching to fit with people's existing desire systems, then you're not doing them any favors and you won't succeed in imparting the Buddha's teachings."

But doesn't his own decision not to handle money affect his capacity to teach? He has to be driven by laypeople wherever he needs to go, they have to buy his plane tickets and meals. "It's not such a hassle, really," he says. "You get used to it. It works. Besides, our supporters enjoy doing that and we never go anywhere we're not invited, except on the traditional *tudong*, or walking tour, where we live on whatever is freely offered to us by the people we meet. If there's an invitation, we might go. If there's no invitation, we stay at home. We don't ever *ask* anyone to take us anywhere."

But what if he's going somewhere and there's no one to meet him at the airport as arranged—how does he deal with situations like that when he can't handle money?

"What's the worst thing that can happen, really?" he asks. "You go without food for a few days. That's not such a big deal in the overall scheme of things."

There's probably little danger of them running out of food at the monastery in Mendocino County. Supporters have so far proved to be so generous that the monastery donates surplus food each week to a local homeless shelter.

## Learning to Give as a Practice

The Buddhist scriptures contain quite explicit guidance on giving. If a monk or lama were giving a sermon in a temple in the East, he'd talk about who we should give to, what we can give, how we should do it and why it's worth doing.

"Charity begins at home." It's no use being generous to strangers if you can't remember your sister's birthday. If you can't be generous to your own friends and relations, then other acts of apparent generosity are likely to miss the point. That's because when we give, as a spiritual practice, we're trying to break down the walls between self and other. Just throwing a check or two over the divide for some good cause won't do it. That doesn't, of course, mean that charity ends at home: it just begins there. Practicing giving is like practicing the Development of Loving-Kindness meditation that we explored in the last chapter. You take your imagination—and your giving—out from yourself to your nearest and dearest, but then learn to extend it so that more and more people become near and dear, or at least more alive in our imagination, more human. Traditional Buddhism tells us to take our practice of giving outward to the sick, the afflicted and the helpless, but not just in a way that gets them off our back.

Giving is a practice we need to engage in fully. Mindlessly dropping a dollar or two into the paper cup a homeless woman holds out to you on the street before you rush by can be less a generous act than a way of defending ourselves from one of life's more difficult realities. Would writing a check to a homeless organization be better? It's good to write a check, but our generosity can go much further. We need to engage ourselves fully in the act. When you next give to someone on the street, stop, if only for two seconds, look them in the eye, greet them and wish them well, give and move on. Giving can bring us into a deeper engagement with life. It shouldn't be a way of buffering ourselves from it.

Take Megan. She really disliked beggars coming up to her in the street. She felt a kind of repugnance at their unwashed state, she felt physically insecure in their presence and deep down they reminded her of where she might end up if things didn't keep going well for her. They also impeded her progress down the street, and Megan always seemed to be in a hurry. But occasionally, she'd throw a few quarters their way to keep them at a distance.

Determined to practice generosity, she decided that she'd have to do something about this. The next time she was accosted by a homeless man on the street she paused and glanced at him, making a quick judgment that he wasn't actually threatening. So she stopped and greeted him, asked him how he was doing, put two dollars in his cup and wished him well. It seemed to go well—the man was polite and his smile seemed genuine enough. The whole process took less than two minutes but it changed Megan's whole orientation to walking about town. Now she feels a little bit less fearful when she goes anywhere. She doesn't feel she has to be so self-protective when it comes to dealing with beggars, and although it may take her two or three more minutes to get where she's going, her life on the street is that much richer.

Megan's story also highlights what we should give. It's not a good idea to start the practice of giving by parting with our whole fortune. As we saw with the Development of Loving-Kindness, it's best to start with what comes easiest: to give what's most readily at hand. That way, we create an attitude of giving. In traditional Buddhist countries, if you call on someone at home it would be unthinkable for them not to offer you something to eat or drink, however humble their circumstances. Many make it a practice to give something every day, getting the habit of giving ingrained into the texture of their normal day-to-day existence, rather than a twice yearly exercise for birthdays and Chanukah or Christmas.

How Megan gave is important. She'd learned that giving is not about throwing those coins and then moving on. We should try to ensure that we give appropriately, what people really need or what they'll enjoy. Not just what we would like them to have because we like it. This requires a degree of imaginative engagement with the person you're giving to. You need to put yourself in their shoes. At the most basic level, we may love Schubert's piano sonatas, but there's no point in giving them to our friend who prefers hip-hop. We should try to be as aware as we can be of the recipient. What do they want? What do they need? And how do they feel about being given to? It's not always easy to give graciously, but don't let that stop you. Think about it. Would you rather receive something clumsily given or nothing at all? Traditional Buddhism says that we should give courteously, happily, quickly and without regret. Agonizing over a donation undoes the meaning of the gift. Better not to give than to feel you were forced into it. Buddhist scriptures also tell us not to draw attention to our own generosity, not to discriminate between friend and foe, or the good person and the so-called evildoer.

That gives us a set of clues about why we should give. It's not just a question of passing money or possessions from one person to another, or giving this to that particular person whom we've singled out for attention. Generosity is an attitude that shapes our whole being: it becomes who we are. The Buddhist ideal is to become so generous that we don't even think of ourselves as generous donors, or think of those we give to as deserving recipients. We just give because that's a part of being fully alive. "When I give," Walt Whitman told us in a line that captures this ideal for us, "I give myself."

That's a high ideal indeed.

## GETTING STARTED

How do we get started? Here are a few things you can do right away that you yourself will enjoy:

- ▾ Send a postcard, today, to someone you know would appreciate hearing from you. You can have some fun choosing the card, writing the message and imagining your friend's pleasure when it arrives.
- ▾ Take some candy in to work tomorrow and share it. Make sure you have a piece for yourself, but also make sure there's enough to go around your work group, even those you don't tend to hang out with.
- ▾ Is there a movie or an exhibition that you'd like to see? Invite a friend to come along with you next week, your treat.

If that seems too easy, try to pick something that's not at the top of your own list but which you know they're likely to enjoy.

Over the next month, buy one or more copies of a book or a CD that you recently enjoyed and give it to someone who you think would like it.

You can think of the practice of giving like throwing a great party. As the host, you are having a brilliant time, not least because you can see all your friends enjoying themselves with each other, and there are all these delighted people who you don't even know but whose happiness you've helped make possible.

Giving is one of the most direct and practical ways of breaking down the barrier between self and other. When we give, and go beyond that barrier for a time, the sense of freedom and expansion that comes from that is deeply enjoyable. Giving is a great pleasure, but it doesn't always come naturally, and as with any skill that we're trying to learn and practice, sometimes we need a little extra encouragement. The benefits that giving brings us can be a rich source of encouragement: when we give, we often get a lot out of it for ourselves directly, and we need to remember this. Getting when we give is all to the good: certainly to begin with.

## Getting When We Give

Let's take the example of Marc Lieberman. Marc is an eye surgeon, practicing in San Francisco, and twice a year, for about nine weeks in all, he voluntarily runs eye camps in Tibet where they practice a simple procedure that saves large numbers of people from blindness. It costs him between $40,000 and $50,000 to be away in Tibet: there's no income during those months but still he has employees and there's rent and insurance to pay for an office that is unused.

"But I can't afford *not* to do this," he says. "I'm getting so much from going to Tibet, at both the profane and the sacred levels. On one level there is a great deal of ego gratification in doing this work. It's part of my identity, and I like being seen by my colleagues and patients to do it. But on a higher level there are the visceral, deeply resonant joys of being there, of observing how, after seven years of showing up in Lhasa for nine weeks a year, the camps are now exclusively conducted by the Tibetans themselves, eliminating preventable blindness among their countrymen in eye camps run in my absence. There's the joy of watching the early fumbling efforts of our joint-cooperative medical project manifest solely because so many cooperative factors and people converged: Chinese administrators, American donors and trainers, Tibetan doctors and nurses, low-level health bureaucrats. And there's the never-get-tired-of joy of witnessing a blind human being open their eyes after surgery to again behold the world of sight and, of all places, in Tibet, which is so redolent with physical splendor!

"I used to imagine that my fifty-, sixty-, seventy-hour work weeks were somehow fixed. I was stuck in fifth gear, working, studying, writing textbooks, doing lectures. Just spending time hanging out was somehow inconceivable to me. I was a *human doing* rather than a *human being*. Now I go to Tibet. It's very hard work physically, working at 15,000 feet usually. I can only sleep four hours a night with so little oxygen, and yet I've discovered there a capacity for living at a slower, more human, pace. In Lhasa one is disengaged from the old familiar media- and entertainment-dominated culture that is totally amalgamated to our Western context of efficiency and productivity. There, I avail myself of the intimate expatriate community to hang out with people, dine and schmooze. It's an opportunity to slow down and be less distracted, to stay out of vehicles and off the phone, to read novels to the end, meet new people, meditate regularly. The old habits of my personality—of dancing so fast to keep up that I get exhausted and out-of-balance in so many ways—are easier to deal with there in the Tibetan/Chinese pace of daily life. So for me the act of giving is, paradoxically, enhanced by my receiving so much in return.

"Every motivation has its complexities, but in the end I do it for the love of being there, and the love of taking the considerable blessings of my birth—being born into a middle-class education-loving, adoring Jewish family in America, and having the best medical education and training—and being able to give back to the world to alleviate suffering in the small area of preventing blindness. That's something I can do. I can't imagine just playing golf instead."

For Marc, the act of giving is deeply, directly enriching.

Under the delusive sway of craving and aversion, we often think that by giving we will be left less well off. Of course, that can be the case if we haven't learned to give as a spiritual practice. A drunk, for example, might give away part of his savings to a group of fellow drinkers and wake up to regret it. But giving can enrich us. It leaves us happier and more free. When it comes to what really matters, the more we give, the richer we become.

## The Hidden Rewards of Giving

Sometimes, the benefits are not obvious. But they are nonetheless very real, if indirect. Even if we don't get something back directly, we'll benefit from creating a climate of generosity around us. This helps create a kind of hidden wealth that we can all share, in the form of knowledge, culture, friendship and other social relations. When we give, we may deplete our store of material goods, but our stock of hidden wealth goes up as we strengthen our friendships and other relationships.

Dominic teaches at the London Business School, where he sometimes asks well-known professors, politicians and business people to come and address his students. They rarely charge a fee. Why should that be? Perhaps it's because they find the experience enjoyable, or maybe they want the students to form a favorable impression of them or their company, or maybe because they'll be able to ask a favor in return one day. In short, they give because they gain. But this can only work if all those involved are willing to participate freely, happily giving to one another because their lives are enriched in the process. If what they want to get becomes too specific, then it turns in a kind of barter system. Imagine if Dominic had to work things out deal by deal: "I'll talk to your students next week if you'll talk to mine in two months' time." That sort of rigidity would kill the system and leave everyone worse off.

We find the same process at work in any successful family, neighborhood or community. I lend you my lawnmower and one day maybe I'll borrow your stepladder. When your car breaks down I give you a ride to the store, and you give me the cup of flour I need for a recipe I'm trying. None of this is negotiated, it's all freely given and it makes all of our lives richer and more pleasant. Generous people are far more likely to receive in their turn than those who are curmudgeonly. They are also happier.

Sonia was feeling miserable at home. Since the kids left, there was no life around the house. She went to work, kept the house clean, spoke on the phone and visited with friends from time to time. But still, there was something missing. Sonia didn't need money, she had enough to get by, but life felt a little flat. But she was still able to notice that a younger work colleague was looking harassed and tired. They had a chat over coffee one day, and Sonia offered to baby-sit once in a while. She's made a good friend: not only that, she's found a whole social circle of younger, lively people.

Two things happened here. Firstly, Sonia increased her stock of hidden wealth. She made a lot of new friends. Secondly, she changed herself. By opening out to others that bit more she became less self-referential. Her world opened up to include others and she became warmer and happier—better to be with.

It can help us to give if we think how much we ourselves have received. We heard about a university professor who invited himself to co-teach a course that a colleague had developed. "I'll need three days of your time so I can get up to speed with your material," he said. His colleague gave him three days of his time. Next, the professor asked that his name be added to the copyright line on all of the materials. "I'd look foolish teaching it with just your name there," he said. Then he started teaching variants of the same course, using his colleague's material in other settings with some success.

Imagine this happening to you. You might feel angry that your work had been stolen. Certainly your colleague had taken what was not freely given. But you could instead reflect on where all the materials that you'd been using for the course had originally come from: they're mostly drawn from the work of others. It's all part of a great stream of knowledge from which you yourself have already received so much. You might well look on that course, at least in part, as a gift to you, that you in turn are passing on. Whatever we have comes from somewhere else. We ourselves have received so much. What can we do but give?

## Auditing Your Generosity

Reflect on ways in which you are already creating hidden wealth. What are they? How might more giving give you more? You might want to audit your giving over the last year or so: there's a simple form in the exercise section of this chapter that will help you do this. We can estimate the money that we gave, and work out to whom we gave it. But there's more that we can give than just money. We could give our possessions: from things we don't need, to objects that we treasure. We can give our labor, as an act of service. We can give time, companionship, love and much more besides.

When you've done your self-audit, you'll find that reflecting on your history of giving bears considerable fruit. Bhikshuni Thubten Chodron, an American-born Buddhist nun, helps her students reflect on their practice of giving by exploring its limits. In keeping with the spirit of generosity, Chodron gave us to use in this book a simple framework that she uses in her discussion groups. She asks her group members what they find easy to give, and what they find difficult to give. Next she asks them to consider whom they're giving to. With whom is it easy? Is there anyone we'd rather not give to? And, all the time, why? "Why" is the crucial question, because it helps us discover what's happening at the frontier of our generosity.

It's great to benefit when we give—directly or indirectly—but to make giving a practice, we can't stay permanently within our comfort zone. We need to find the frontier: that point where our practice of giving is just starting to cause us to say "ouch!" Athletes like tennis players, sometimes talk about finding the sweet-spot. That's the perfect point on a tennis racket from which you can make the perfect stroke. You feel it right through your body. That point at which we are just starting to say "ouch!" in our practice of giving is the sweet-spot of generosity. By keeping our game of giving in the sweet-spot, we'll start to extend our practice of generosity, changing who we are into a more generous person.

## Finding the Sweet-Spot

Martin Babson bravely agreed to let us help him find his sweet-spot.

Martin is a successful lawyer who gives away quite a lot. He was able to do the first part of his self-audit quite quickly. In his last financial year, he gave away about 15 percent of his earnings. Some of that was regular giving through ongoing monthly payments from his bank account. That includes $3,000 a year to his local Buddhist center, and another $9,000 to two non-Buddhist charities that provide assistance to disadvantaged or homeless youngsters. He'd given away the fees arising from a semi-charitable legal project that he'd initiated in his spare time: that was about $30,000 over the year. And he'd given away another $3,000 as particular needs arose. For example, an artist friend needed funding for a website, and

Martin decided to support a monk on a long solitary retreat. Possessions? He'd inherited furniture from an aunt, and was lending some of the pieces to an old friend. "Lend?" we asked. "Well, I'm calling it a loan, but I don't expect to ever get them back. We wouldn't have room for them at home anyway." Martin gives his labor. He and his wife donate their Sunday mornings twice a month helping to prepare meals for homebound invalids, and he's also a trustee of the charity that provides this service through a network of kitchens and distribution hubs across a major urban area. He struggled with some of the other parts of his self-audit, but realized that he gave a lot of time (that he didn't have to give) to colleagues and junior associates in his law firm. "And I could talk about companionship and love too, I guess, but that makes me cringe a bit, because that just doesn't feel like giving."

Once Martin had told us the results of his self-audit, we started to peel back the layers of his generosity using Chodron's framework, starting with what he found easiest. "Giving money is quite easy, certainly for now while I've got quite a lot. But my income's likely to fall when the recession deepens. Perhaps that'll be the real test. I know I'd feel really ashamed if I stopped my regular giving plans while we were still eating out regularly in nice restaurants." The work he does as a volunteer with his wife is very close to Martin's heart. "I feel privileged being able to do something like this. Of course there are times when I don't feel like getting out of bed on a Sunday morning to chop vegetables, but we've both gotten so much out of it. We've made new friends, and one of my fellow trustees has put some business my way. There can be a great atmosphere in the kitchen too. Sometimes it's a heck of a lot of fun." We asked Martin how he'd originally become involved. His wife's mother had been one of this Sunday meal service's beneficiaries before her death some years before. "We'd been given something, and we wanted to put something back."

We asked him whether he'd had second thoughts about any of the causes or people that he supports. "Not really," he said. "I guess

I only tend to give money to people and causes that strike a strong chord with me. The Buddhist center's kind of like my own home: it would feel odd not to give it money. The two charities for teenage kids? Well, an old friend's son got into drugs and then became a runaway at seventeen. Giving to those kids feels like giving to that one: I really want to help. I have to charge the legal helpline because my law partnership is involved. I'd normally do something like that for free, so I'm just giving away a windfall. My artist friend? I've bought one or two of his paintings. They're really great and I'd like to see others enjoy his work, but he's so un-businesslike. Hopefully the website will work as an easy way for folks to learn about him.

"It was harder giving to the monk," said Martin. "The amount of money wasn't all that much, but it was quite an effort to get my head around helping the guy to disappear for eighteen months on solitary retreat. With him going, we've lost a great meditation teacher. I can't say that I know the guy well. I guess I just had to take it on faith that something good would happen." He doesn't like being hassled for money, and almost always ignores charitable appeals, or contributes only a small amount. "I like choosing what to give to: being asked puts me on the spot in a way that I frankly find uncomfortable."

Martin reckons that parting with money is easier than giving away possessions. "I've kept some kind of claim even on things I don't want, like my aunt's stuff. It's a long time since I parted with something that I really treasure." Although Martin is generous with his time, and takes a lot of pleasure in giving advice and career counseling, he hates having it wasted. "Time is so precious. If I give it to someone, I do want to know that it's valued." He admitted to some annoyance at the time it was taking his artist friend to get photos of his portfolio to the website designer. "Sometimes I wonder whether the guy's taking the help I've given him seriously," Martin said. We talked about some of the other expectations many people have when they give: getting something material in return, receiving praise, love, acceptance or gaining reputation and power.

Martin shook his head. None of those rang any bells for him. "But I guess what I do expect in return is appreciation, not so much of me, as of what I've given."

If Martin wants to extend his practice of generosity into the sweet-spot, he might try giving away a possession once in a while. Not his most treasured family heirloom, but something of his own that he values, to someone whom he really cares about (because it's easier to give to those we love most). He seems to like retaining a strongly potent connection when he gives, even staying in control. Once in a while, he might consider responding to an appeal from a charity or individual that hadn't figured on his giving plan, and, while giving, learn more about it. He might, for example, make an extra effort to understand why solitary retreats are so important to monks and others who teach meditation. That way, he'll gently stretch his already considerable capacity for generosity, and as he expands the ways he gives he'll extend his scope for empathy.

You too might want to apply Chodron's framework to peel back the layers of giving in your own life. We've seen how Martin worked through it. Why not complete this simple analysis for yourself?

## TRY THIS:
Write down the answers to these questions, being specific:

What have you given in the last year?
- ▾ *time?*
- ▾ *money?*
- ▾ *possessions?*
- ▾ *service?*
- ▾ *love?*
- ▾ *companionship?*
- ▾ *anything else?*

What do you find easy to give?
What do you find difficult to give?

Whom is it easy to give to?

Whom is it difficult to give to?

What, inside you, makes it difficult to give to others?

- ▾ *Do you feel it's making a show?*
- ▾ *Is it miserliness?*
- ▾ *Is it difficult to express affection to others?*
- ▾ *Is it fear of rejection?*
- ▾ *What else might it be?*

What kind of expectations do you find yourself having when you give?

- ▾ *Do you expect to receive something material in return?*
- ▾ *Do you expect to receive praise?*
- ▾ *Do you expect to receive love?*
- ▾ *Do you expect to gain power?*
- ▾ *Do you expect to gain acceptance into a group?*
- ▾ *Do you expect to gain an enhanced reputation?*
- ▾ *Anything else?*

What do your answers to these questions tell you about yourself? Which of these things might be easy to change? Which might be difficult?

Start with the easy issues and make a plan to change them. If you find it hard to give to someone you don't like, think of a way to give something to such a person. If you find you always expect to get a gift in return, try to give something with no thought of receiving. Do that a few times. Then have another look at the questions. Has anything changed? Again, pick off a few easy targets and make a plan to do something about them. This will help you, like Martin, move into the sweet-spot of giving.

## Overcoming Conflicts

Chodron herself is trying to work on her own sweet-spot. But it's not always easy, even for a highly experienced spiritual practitioner. Any of us, Chodron says, can get caught up in conflicts when we set out to give. Sometimes we almost have to force ourselves to act in order to break through the flack of mental chatter our reactive minds throw up when an act of generosity looms.

She told us a story that illustrates the kinds of conflict we often get into when we set out to give. Monks and nuns are usually the recipients of other people's generosity, but Chodron likes to give as well. Like all of us, she has sometimes encountered difficulties in this area.

As a nun, clothed in traditional maroon robes, she is restricted in what she can wear. Getting maroon sweaters, jackets and coats to go over her robes can be difficult, because they can't be found in ordinary shops every year. Once, while teaching Buddhism in Japan, her friends gave her a maroon cashmere sweater. Not only was it that prized color, but cashmere is so soft and nice to wear. She loved the sweater.

A year or two after that, she was on a teaching tour in the former Soviet republics and, as winter was just ending there, she had the sweater with her. She and her translator arrived in Kiev one morning. Since their train wasn't leaving for Donetsk until the evening, Igor, the translator, called his friend Sasha and they spent the day at her flat. Sasha was a young woman who had very little: Ukraine, where Kiev is located, is one of the most impoverished regions in Europe. She served them various forms of potatoes for lunch and dinner and she shared around some sweets that she'd been saving.

In the subway heading to the main Kiev rail station that evening, an idea popped into Chodron's mind. As she puts it, there was a voice saying: "Give Sasha the sweater." But immediately, another part of her mind said "No way!" and a civil war ensued all the way to the station. "She'd love it!" "But if you give it, you'll be cold." "You're so stingy. She has nothing and has been so generous with you." "Don't be so sentimental. It'll be summer soon and she won't need it." And on and on the voices went. They arrived at the train station and Sasha went to get some special buns for them to eat on the train. Chodron's internal dialogue continued. "Look, she's spending what little money she has. You have so much. Give her the sweater." "It's in the bottom of the suitcase. It'd create a mess to pull it out now. Forget it."

Once on the train Chodron put her suitcase under the seat. Sasha sat with them as they waited for the train to leave. The civil war raged on. Finally, Chodron reached under the seat, into the suitcase. She pulled out the sweater and gave it to Sasha whose face lit up in a way that Chodron had never seen before. She was so happy! Chodron kicked herself that she'd been so reluctant and stingy. The train started to move and they said good-bye. Chodron returned to Kiev a few weeks later. Sasha met her at the train station. She was wearing the sweater, even though it was warm spring weather. "I determined," Chodron said, "to try never to miss an opportunity to give. I haven't always been able to keep to that, but the memory of Sasha's happiness at receiving the sweater sticks in my mind."

We have all probably experienced that kind of internal conflict when it comes to giving, and often it prevents us from doing what, in the deepest part of us, we know is best. But reflect on the benefits of giving and, as they said in the Nike ads, Just do it. It can be a wrench, but the more often we give, the better we get at doing it.

## Giving and Receiving

As well as having difficulties with giving, we can sometimes have difficulties with receiving and the two can be quite closely related.

If we can't receive graciously it's going to be harder to give graciously, for the issues that we have with receiving will also affect our giving.

One of Chodron's Tibetan teachers, Zong Rinpoche was visiting Los Angeles, and some people wanted to take him to Disneyland. Americans love taking the lamas to Disneyland and Chodron very much wanted to go along because she learns a lot by being with her own teachers in those kind of informal situations. The trouble was, she had no money.

She casually let it be known that she didn't have enough money but would like to go. "As a group of us were talking, one man came up and offered to sponsor me so that I could go. Now as soon as he did this, I thought about my motivation and realized that I had been dropping hints. I felt awful for being conniving and deceptive, only thinking about my own pleasure! So I refused. I just couldn't accept."

A few minutes later, another of her teachers, Geshe Gyaltsen, who had observed all of this, asked her, "Why didn't you let him pay for your trip?"

"Geshe-la," she replied, "I had a rotten motivation. I wasn't being straightforward."

"When somebody wants to be generous with you," said Geshe Gyaltsen, "you should accept their generosity and then change your motivation. You shouldn't deny them the joy and merit they receive from giving. But you shouldn't neglect to change your motivation either."

Chodron shared with us her own approach to understanding our difficulties in accepting others' generosity. What light do her questions shed on your attitude to others' gifts to you?

## TRY THIS: HOW DO WE RECEIVE?

What have you been given in the last year?
- ▾ *Time?*
- ▾ *Money?*
- ▾ *Possessions?*
- ▾ *Service?*
- ▾ *Love?*
- ▾ *Companionship?*
- ▾ *What else?*

What did you find easy to accept?
What do you find difficult to receive?
Who is it easy to receive from?
Who is it difficult to receive from?
Why is it difficult for you to receive? What blocks you?
- ▾ *Do you feel undeserving?*
- ▾ *Do you feel that you'll be obligated to the person giving?*
- ▾ *Do you fear that the other person may try to manipulate you?*
- ▾ *What else?*

Next time someone offers to give you something, reflect on how that makes you feel. Did you try to avoid receiving what the other person wanted to give? Think about how you're blocking their generous impulse and try not to do that again.

▾   ▾   ▾

It's important to allow people to give and it's important to be able to receive. The precept of generosity is not just to do with our own capacity for giving. It's ultimately about making the world a more generous place, without distinction between self and other.

If we are particularly fortunate in terms of our opportunities to give, then we have a special responsibility to consider others' capacity to receive.

## Considering the Recipient

Kulamitra has had to learn a great deal about helping people to receive. His story is a little unusual but still has lessons for us all.

His mother's family is very wealthy. He received a small inheritance from his grandfather when he turned twenty-one, but there was much more to come. A trust fund had been set up for the whole family, and over the years Kulamitra was to benefit from this substantially. It meant that he never had to work for his living, and that he had many opportunities to give to his friends and to support causes and projects—almost exclusively Buddhist—that he cared about strongly with his money and time.

But it wasn't always easy for the recipients.

In his early twenties, Kulamitra had chosen to live in a residential Buddhist community in Norwich, England. His fellow community members had little or no money, and by comparison, Kulamitra—even with his small initial inheritance—was very rich indeed. This community operated a common purse. A common purse is exactly that: you each put all of your money into it, and all community members then take from it what they need. The idea behind this was first to allow everyone to practice sharing, and secondly to leave them free to devote their energies to spiritual practice and to helping out at the local Buddhist center. In this case, however, since Kulamitra was the only one with any money, only he was paying into the common purse, while everybody else was taking from it. "This could be very hard for us at times," one of his fellow community members told us, looking back after many years. "It didn't feel as if the purse was ours collectively. We kept on asking Kulamitra for permission whenever we needed something like a new pair of jeans. Maybe we weren't mature enough in those days. It was weird receiving so much from one person." It was also, he said, hard on Kulamitra. "Here was this guy being so generous. He'd given the community all his money, but there we were, behaving as if he hadn't actually given it. We kept on and on hassling him to tell us how it should be spent. We just couldn't take the responsibility."

Giving unwisely nearly cost him friendships. Kulamitra made a substantial interest-free loan to get a Buddhist project off the ground. "The business plan unraveled, they couldn't repay me by the due date and communication started to break down." Another time, he lent money to a close friend. Similar problems cropped up. "What was so painful was that this guy started to avoid me. Then I felt we had to cut through all of this, so I just gave him the money: I wrote off the loan. Incredibly, that made things much, much worse. He was distant for a time after that. The way I went about things must have humiliated him. That taught me a lot about how to give, and how not to."

Today, Kulamitra is an experienced Buddhist teacher. We asked him if he had any special advice for readers of this book. Here are his suggestions on how to give well:

1. Do not be pressured into giving or lending.
2. Make a real decision—keep the initiative.
3. Don't be afraid to give to what you love.
4. Once you give, let go.
5. Just live with your original decision, whatever comes.

He also shared his practical insights on the pitfalls of giving:

1. Never lend more than you can afford to lose.
2. Better not lend to a friend—just give what they need.
3. Don't give from guilt, but from love.
4. Listen to your friends, but make your own judgment.
5. Giving should increase peace of mind, not undermine it.

You might want to consider your own recent acts of generosity in relation to Kulamitra's suggestions. How could you be more skillful in the way you give?

Edward Conze, one of the great Western Buddhist scholars of the twentieth century, reminds us that we are very privileged to be able to give, and need to practice humility when we do so. We need to bear in mind that it is we ourselves who are the greatest beneficiaries of our own generosity, and so give with special care so that our giving does not harm those who receive.

## The Cultivation of Generosity

You might like to spend a little time reflecting imaginatively on yourself as giver, on what you might give and on those you might give to. Our imagination is an extraordinarily powerful tool for use in spiritual development, for it can conjure up what we aspire to be in full Technicolor. It can take us from words to pictures, from ideas to heartfelt emotions. That future state to which we aspire, for all that it may be far, far away, will start to become real and our energy and enthusiasm for transformation will awaken.

Try this practice, which we've adapted from the meditation on Loving-Kindness to which we introduced you in the last chapter. It's not a traditional Buddhist practice, but it can have very beneficial effects.

As we saw before, preparation is a key to effective meditation. The room should be peaceful: pick a time for ten or twenty minutes when the kids (or anyone else) won't burst in on you as you try to reflect. We suggest spending a few minutes, before you begin the practice, to find a sitting posture that allows you to be both comfortable and alert. If you choose to sit on a chair, pick one that's firm and that allows you to sit with your spine naturally erect. Let your feet rest uncrossed on the floor. Feel the weight of your legs, the weight of the body and the contact it makes with your chair or meditation mat. You might settle into yourself by spending a little while listening to your breath, taking in its rise and fall much as you might watch and listen to the waves when you're at the ocean.

We have all been given many wonderful things in the course of our lives. Try to recall some of what you've been given that you value most. We won't be able to remember everything, of course, but consider for a few moments how well-off you are thanks to the generosity of others. Those others might be your parents, your life partner, your friends, co-workers. Ever since we got the gift of life at the beginning, people have been giving to us. With the imagination, we might replay some particular moments when we were especially moved by someone's gift. How did it feel? We can let our mind dwell on those feelings, letting them expand.

Now start to give things away. Bring a good friend to mind and imagine that you're giving things to him or her. In our imagination, we can safely give away anything we like, without fear of regretting it later, so why not be adventurous and up the stakes? If you're already very generous to your close friends, give more! What gift would your closest friend appreciate most? What is your own most prized possession? Try giving it to your friend in your imagination, and see what happens, what feelings are produced by this purely imaginary act of giving.

Then, as we did in the Loving-Kindness practice in the last chapter, call to mind someone you don't care about either way, and then a difficult person whom you know. Imagine yourself giving freely and bounteously to all of them. You can go through the things you'd like to be able to give them: money, possessions, time, affection. Just imagine yourself giving. Imagine what it would be like for them to receive all of these good things. What feelings do you encounter as you imagine giving freely, with no hindrance?

Then you can allow your generosity to extend outward, further and further, giving to more and more people until eventually it encompasses all living beings everywhere. Just keep on giving. Open your heart and feel the delight and freedom that comes from wholehearted generosity.

Here is a step-by-step summary of the practice:

TRY THIS: THE CULTIVATION OF GENEROSITY

Get into the meditation posture that suits you and relax. When you feel ready, start with stage one. Try devoting about five minutes to each stage to begin with. You can extend that as you grow more used to meditation.

Stage One: Call to mind all the wonderful things that you have or have received from others. You won't be able to call *everything* to mind, but consider for a few moments how well-off you are. Your parents gave to you, your partner has, your friends and relatives have, society has. You've received so much generosity over time and now you're quite well-off in many ways.

Stage Two: Begin to give things away. Call to mind a good friend, and imagine that you're giving things to him or her— money, possessions, time, affection—whatever comes to mind. Just imagine yourself giving. Imagine what it would be like for them to receive all of these good things. Notice the feelings you encounter as you imagine giving freely, with no hindrance.

Stage Three: Call to mind a neutral person and imagine giving to them, just as freely as you gave to your friend.

State Four: Call to mind an enemy, or someone with whom your communication is currently rather difficult and imagine yourself giving freely and bounteously to him. Just imagine yourself giving and giving freely, with no hindrance, no feelings of regret.

Stage Five: Allow your generosity to extend outward, further and further, until eventually it encompasses all living beings everywhere. Just keep on giving. Open your heart and feel the delight and freedom that comes from wholehearted generosity.

When you draw the practice to a close, resolve to give something definite to someone definite that very day.

For all that this practice is nontraditional, like generosity itself it has the essence of Buddhism at its heart. Limitless generosity— with no distinction between giver and recipient, where giving is so universal and spontaneous that we can't even point out a particular generous act—is the Buddhist aspiration. As the Mahayana Buddhist teacher Shantideva puts it:

> Just as the earth and other elements,
> Are serviceable in many ways
> To the infinite number of beings
> Inhabiting limitless space:
> So may I become
> That which maintains all beings
> Situated throughout space
> So long as all have not attained to peace.[15]

## Transforming Self and World

The transformational power of generosity goes beyond ourselves to ignite a chain reaction as others respond to what is given to them. It opens up the Path of Abundance for others as well as for ourselves.

As we have seen, giving money and possessions is only a start, to get us going. In traditional Buddhist discussions of generosity, there are more and higher levels of giving. At the very top of the list comes the gift of understanding reality. Next is the gift of merit: that encapsulates the idea that we can give away our own goodness, so that others will benefit from it. Then comes the gift of education and culture.

In between these very refined kinds of giving and the gift of material things comes the gift of confidence: of giving fearlessness to others. In fearful times, like times of conflict, it's easy to see that many people—quite apart from those who have suffered terrible personal loss—are very, very worried. Faces appear tense and

---

15. Verses from Shantideva's *Bodhicharya-avatara* as used in the FWBO Puja Book (Birmingham, England: Windhorse Publications, 2000).

strained. Strangers, especially those from different nationalities or ethnic groups, sometimes have fear in their eyes when they glance at us on our city subways. When a whole people comes to live under the influence of fear there is an oppressive cloud over the land. Trust diminishes, confidence in each other is lost, we shrink from each other, retreat into enclosed private worlds and enlarge the gulf between self and other. Our task, as we practice generosity, is to undo that.

Those who know Buddhist art might recall one of the classic representations of the Buddha, that you can see in the great statues of the Buddha that are still to be found in Asia. This is the representation of the Buddha as he gives the gift of fearlessness, holding out his hand, palm toward us, saying "Have no fear." This is the spirit that we ourselves might embody as we give. By giving, even just a little, we will perceptibly lighten the darkness that we all live in, because our giving will be saying: "Yes. We can make a difference. We can be potent. You and I and anyone can do something to break down the barriers that divide. Be confident and less afraid."

# SIX

## The Third Precept: Cultivate Contentment

*Avoid sexual misconduct, cultivate contentment.*

*Health is the highest gain, contentment the greatest riches.*[16]

The third precept is traditionally formulated in terms of refraining from sexual misconduct, and the positive counterpart to sexual misconduct is the cultivation of sexual contentment. But if we look at the root meaning of the term that is translated from the Pali as "sexual" we find that it means "to desire," or "to enjoy," which goes beyond the common meaning of the term.

At its most essential, this precept is about learning to deal with our passions, with our desire for stimulation, intensity and excitement. So, especially when we're looking at it from the perspective of money, this precept can be taken to mean that we should avoid misconduct by way of craving, or sensual enjoyment. And just as the positive counterpart to sexual misconduct is the cultivation of sexual contentment, so the positive counterpart to the precept in-

---

16. Trans. Sangharakshita, *Dhammapada: The Way of Truth*, v. 204 (Birmingham, England: Windhorse Publications, 2001).

terpreted more essentially is the cultivation of contentment in its most general form.

Suzuki Roshi, founder of the San Francisco Zen Center, is one of the founding fathers of Zen in America. He arrived in California rather late in life, having first trained for many years under different Zen masters in Japan. One of his foremost teachers was the great master Gempo Kitano-roshi, a man of immense decorum. In a talk one day, Kitano addressed the monks at his monastery, the famous Eiheiji, on the topic of smoking, which most of them did. He never told them not to smoke, but he described his own relationship to tobacco.[17] He was out begging one day and sat down in a pleasant spot above the town to smoke a cigarette. He got tremendous enjoyment from that cigarette—he loved the taste of tobacco in damp weather and he enjoyed watching the smoke drifting and mingling with the mist. Gazing at the town through the haze, Kitano decided that it was such a perfect moment of enjoyment that it was exactly the right time to quit smoking—and so he did.

Commenting further on this story, Suzuki Roshi said that although Kitano Roshi stopped smoking, he never lost the desire to smoke—but he knew "how to treat his desires." "I don't tell you that you shouldn't smoke," he added, "but you would be foolish not to pay attention to this story."

The third precept is about learning how to treat our desires. As we have seen, our desires go to the very heart of who we are. They shape and define us. What we take, what we push out, under the sway of craving and aversion make us what we now are. And, as we have also seen, there are two kinds of desire: skillful or unskillful, reactive or creative. With this precept, we train ourselves in checking our unskillful, reactive desires in order to make space for skillful, creative desires to flourish.

The root of all reactive desires is the deep, but often barely

---

17. See David Chadwick, *Crooked Cucumber: The Life and Zen Teaching of Shunryu Suzuki* (New York: Broadway Books, 1999).

conscious sense we have that somewhere, somehow, we are currently incomplete. There is a hole, deep in the center of each one of us, that we try to fill with sensory experience. Whether it's a chocolate bar, a cigarette, a new car, more money or the perfect vacation, there's always something out there that we think will make us complete.

Perhaps you've had an experience like this. You're working at your job, or you're out for a walk, or talking with a friend, and you start to feel slightly uneasy. You're not quite comfortable with things. There's something missing, something you're not getting—something's not quite right in your life. Gradually, this feeling builds in intensity and then suddenly, it erupts into full and glorious awareness. "Yes!" you think. "I know what it is. I know what's not right. I need a Snickers! Of course." And so the thought of a Snickers bar starts to grow in your mind, it sort of throbs and glows there—Snickers, Snickers, Snickers. It's now really hard to concentrate on what you're doing as images of chocolate and candy float and dance in your mind. You can almost taste one—that sharp tang of sweetness, the warm afterglow of chocolate. The desire for that Snickers just builds and builds, until you seem to have no choice. You saunter down to the newsstand, buy one, unwrap it, take a bite and . . . Well, what did you expect? Nirvana? With a feeling of mild disappointment, you return to what you were doing.

Snickers bars, of course, are relatively harmless. They don't do our teeth any good, or our waistline, and they mess with our insulin levels, but on the larger scale of things none of that's disaster. Where we really suffer is when our whole lives are driven by materialism and the urge to consume.

No other modern people have consumed as much as we do today, and none have been so discontented. There are many apparent causes for our discontent—social fragmentation, the breakdown of the traditional family, the pace of change, the loss of religious belief and our constant subjection to brand advertising, to name a few—

but the real issue is that deep down, at a part of our being we're barely conscious of, lies a sense of our own incompleteness. There is no fixed and unchanging essence that we can point to and say "That is me, that is what I truly am." Yet we crave above all simply *to be*, to be whole, to be complete, to be real.

Advertisers tell us that we can achieve this by wearing their brand, or driving it, or drinking it: "Coke—it's the real thing!" But we cannot be made whole, *ever*, and so long as we believe we can, we carry on consuming, chasing after an elusive satisfaction that the world seems to promise. "I shop, therefore I am."

In the film *American Beauty,* Carolyn, the desperate, strained, materialistic wife of Lester, the film's hero, ruins a romantic embrace, and her one hope of reconciliation with her husband, by warning him not to spill his beer on the sofa. "It's just a couch!" he shouts. "It's a $4,000 sofa upholstered in Italian silk!" she shouts back, and with that effectively puts an end to their relationship. What makes this scene particularly poignant is that just for a moment we saw Carolyn dropping her façade, loosening her frenetic grip on life and becoming softer and more loving. For a second or two her humanity shone through. Then she lost it and was absorbed once more into the fierce, cold world of acquisition.

Carolyn's tragedy doesn't consist simply in the fact that she likes her sofas upholstered in Italian silk. Rather it is that her values have been turned upside down and a $4,000 sofa has come to mean more to her than the husband she once loved. The all-pervasive consumerism and materialism of our society undermines our humanity and robs the world we move in of warmth and depth. On a superficial reading, there is nothing really wrong with Carolyn's love of her furniture or her Mercedes car, or with her desperate aspiration to become a star real estate agent. But when we see what her brittle ambitions do to her relationships with her husband and daughter (who play their own parts in the family's dysfunction), then we see the profound ethical consequences of her materialism: it robs her world of life.

The point of the third precept is not that we have to give up candy bars, our liking for good furniture and all our other little (and often not so little) indulgences. Rather, this precept is concerned with bringing awareness to the business of consumption, with getting the material aspect of our lives into proportion, and with learning to maintain our humanity and creativity in the context of the consumer society.

Whether we have a lot or a little, we're all subject to the pressures of consumerism in the developed world today. Wherever we go we receive messages whose sole purpose is to get us to consume. Small wonder, therefore, that we so often find ourselves falling into states of craving. "If only I had . . . a new car / a new refrigerator / a new computer / a new hi-fi / the latest jacket / a home on the beach / a place in the country / a vacation in Venice . . . then I'd be satisfied." But of course it doesn't work, because no sooner do you get what you want than your desire moves on and finds another hook to hang itself on.

TRY THIS:
Think about how much you've consumed this week.

- ▾ What did you spend your money on?
- ▾ How much of it was spent on things you don't really need?
- ▾ How much was spent on things you now realize that you neither want nor need?

If you want to learn to "treat your desires" you have first of all to develop a greater degree of awareness in relation to them. Rather than blindly stumbling on from one moment of consumption to the next you need to pause and reflect—what are you actually doing when you consume? What are you really looking for? All too often, the things we buy don't give us what we expected from them because we weren't fully aware of what those expectations were.

TRY THIS:

Consider a recent purchase you made, say for more than two hundred dollars, and answer the following questions:

- ▾ Besides the object itself, what were you expecting to get from the purchase?
    - ▾ Were you expecting to gain pride from it?
    - ▾ Or pleasure?
    - ▾ Comfort?
    - ▾ Happiness?
    - ▾ An end to your desire?
- ▾ How did you feel at the moment when you actually bought it?
- ▾ How did you feel the day after you bought it? How did you feel the month after you bought it? How do you feel about it now?
- ▾ Were your expectations in relation to the purchase actually met?

Let's look at the story of Joshua, who discovered the pressing need for a new computer, and see how he would have gone about this exercise.

Joshua subscribes to a range of computer magazines. "I need to keep up with the latest developments in IT," he says. "In business today you really can't let yourself fall behind." True enough. But it is also true that he rather likes the mild titillation of it all, the thrill of the new. In odd moments he finds himself leafing through one or another magazine, idly passing the time, when suddenly an article or an ad catches his attention in exactly the way its creator intended it to—

"Wow!" he thinks to himself. "That new Pentium 4 processor is really something! If we had one of those we could do our work so much quicker!"

Well, he says something like that, but really he's just attracted by the new color screen and by the idea of having the very latest, the most powerful, new computer.

"It will make us so much more efficient. I know cash-flow is tight right now, but you've got to invest for the future. We can't fall behind."

And this idea takes root in the back of his mind. In quiet moments it comes back to him and he gives it a little more room—

"Hmm. I really would like one of those new Pentiums 4s. This old Pentium 3 is so clunky. . . . It's really out of date."

After all, it is *two* years old!

And so this idea builds and builds and soon Joshua finds himself in the grip of an obsession, his mind dominated by the desire for a new toy to play with. He tells himself all sorts of stories to rationalize his desire and he spends his spare moments wondering how to free up a bit more capital so that he can go off and buy the thing. He's fallen into the grip of "techno-lust."

So finally Joshua frees up the necessary capital and, joy of joys, calls up the mail-order company and orders the sparkling new computer with next-day delivery (he can't wait). The van drives up, they unload the box, Joshua opens it, discards all the waste packaging and calls the company to get them to send the power-cord that had been left out of the box. That arrives three frustrating days later and he sets up the machine. He tries to load his software, and it crashes. Several increasingly angry calls to the customer service hotline follow—

"If you wish to speak to one of our technical support experts, press '9.' Thank you. Calls are answered in strict rotation. You are fifteenth in line. Your call is important to us. Please hold. . . ."

Ten desperate days after first opening the box, Joshua finally manages to get the machine to work more or less as it should. And yes, it completes some tasks a few seconds faster than the old one did. He'll probably save several whole minutes in the course of a working day.

Somewhere in the pit of his stomach a hollow feeling of dissatisfaction lurks, waiting for the next passing desire to hold out the hope of final satisfaction.

If he'd been honest with himself, this is how Joshua would have responded to the questions we raised in this exercise:

What are you expecting to get from the purchase?

*Increased efficiency*

*Potency*

*Pride*

*Satisfaction*

*Happiness*

How did you feel at the moment when you actually bought it?

*Elated*

*Apprehensive (would it really deliver what it promised?)*

How did you feel the day after you bought it?

*Angry and frustrated*

How did you feel the month after you bought it?

*Indifferent and dissatisfied again*

Were your expectations in relation to the purchase actually met?

*Not really*

And that last question is the true "bottom line." Our expectations with regard to consumption are often not actually met because, in reality, they can't be.

There is a place in this world for new computers, just as there is for Carolyn's $4,000 sofa upholstered in Italian silk. But so long as our consumption is based on unrealistic expectations it is bound to let us down. Carolyn's sofa could never, ever, under any circumstances provide her with the happiness or the security she sought. It cannot, because what she was looking for, underneath it all, was a sense of true being: a sense that she was real, that she mattered, that she counted for something in this world because of what she possessed. Sofas cannot give us that. Nothing can. We have to learn to recognize and go beyond the desire for security itself. Nothing whatsoever can keep the winds of change at bay. Rather than fighting this fact, we can instead learn to love it. Everything always changes. This can be a source of profound insecurity—it can also be the basis of joy and freedom.

In *American Beauty*, Lester is shot and killed after a moment of profound realization and he speaks the closing words of the movie from beyond this life.

He could be pretty mad about what happened to him, he tells us, but that's not easy when there's so much beauty in the world. Sometimes he feels like he's seeing it all at once and it's too much for him, his heart fills up like a balloon that's about to burst. But when that happens he reminds himself to relax, to stop trying to hold on, and then it all flows through him like rain and he can't feel anything but gratitude for every moment of his "stupid little life."

So much of our consumption stems from a desire simply to be here now, fully alive in this moment. But rather than trying to get there by buying things, we can short-circuit the process and get there by dropping our neurotic desires and waking up to the feel of the breeze on our cheek and the warmth of the sun on our arms. Just attending to simple, fleeting sensations we can experience the wonder and beauty of simply being alive. The monetization and commodification of all aspects of our lives deadens us to the beauty of life itself.

Once, in the course of a walk in Kalimpong, a small town in the Himalayan foothills, our teacher, Sangharakshita, came upon a beautiful pine tree. It was a superb specimen, with a thick trunk, absolutely straight, going up for fifty or sixty feet, and with gracefully spreading green branches. He stood looking up at that splendid sight when a Nepali acquaintance of his happened to pass by.

"Look at this beautiful tree!" Sangharakshita exclaimed. "Isn't it magnificent?"

"Yes," his acquaintance replied, "there must be at least three cartloads of firewood there!"

The third precept tells us to give up the less—mindless consumption—for the sake of the more—an increased quality of life. To the extent that we view the world in terms of what we can have, what we can use, what we can own and what we can consume, we live relatively impoverished lives, focusing on the mean, self-referential dimension of our experience and forsaking our access to the deeper world of joy and sorrow that makes up the human realm and from which we can aspire to true liberation.

The Buddha never advocated simplicity and reduced consumption as an end in itself. He advocated it as a means toward a greater happiness. In the Lotus Sutra, he tells a story about a house that burned down. An elder, a very wealthy man, once lived in an old, decaying mansion. He had thirty children and one day, while he was outside, the house caught fire and the children, unaware of the danger, kept on playing their various games inside, making no effort to escape. The elder shouted to them to come out but, engrossed in their games, they ignored him. Realizing that he wouldn't have the time to carry them out one at a time, he hit upon a ruse. "Come out," he called, "and see all the different toys I've bought you. There are all kinds of carts. Some pulled by deer, some pulled by goats, some by bullocks . . ." And the children came rushing out, tumbling over one another in their hurry to get at the new toys. "Where are the carts?" they demanded. And not wanting to disappoint them, the elder gave them each a large bullock cart, much larger and grander than the ones he'd promised them.

There are many different ways in which this story can be interpreted, but we could think of the elder as the Buddha and ourselves as the children, engrossed in our games of getting and spending while the world all around us is blazing with the fires of craving, aversion and delusion. The Buddha calls us to come out, but we ignore him. Realizing that we don't act if we're just called on to deny something we think of as pleasurable, the Buddha instead holds out to us the great pleasures of his path. "Come," he says, "and experience the joys of meditation and spiritual fellowship. Delight in the pleasure of increased awareness and positive emotion. Enjoy the peace of contentment." Putting aside our lesser pleasures for the sake of greater ones, we leave the house, and then we discover that what the Buddha was holding out all the time was the greatest pleasure of all—complete self-transcendence.

Buddhism, the Vietnamese teacher Thich Nhat Hanh said, "is a clever way to enjoy your life." By contrast, emphasizing the quantitative aspects of consumption (how much I have) over the qualitative aspects (how alive I am) is a foolish way.

## Dealing with Our Own Consumerism

Here we are, faced with our consumerist culture, steeped in a consumerist conditioning that, for many of us, runs very deep. What can we do about it?

On the broadest front we begin by becoming more aware of how and why we want what we do. We can then ask ourselves how realistic our expectations are in relation to the things we desire. But that is only the start, because controlling our craving, "taking care of our desires" is not easy. Once a desire has lodged itself in our minds it spreads like a virus, rapidly infecting other parts of our being with its insistent clamor. Joshua glanced at an article in a computer magazine. Just a few hours later he was immersed in an obsessive process of scheming how to buy a new machine. Our desires spread and colonize our minds with ease because, as we've already seen, to a large extent we *are* simply the product of our desires. But so long as we constantly give way to reactive desires, such as the desire to have and to own, then our more creative desires—our yearning for what is truly good—will be weakened, and we'll lead less creative lives.

Dealing with mental disturbances such as craving has always been an issue for Buddhist practitioners. Call to mind an image of the Buddha. What do you see? Most of us will imagine a man sitting calmly immersed in profound meditation. It all seems so easy, so serene and, for the Buddha, it is. But his state of calm serenity was only achieved after a great deal of hard work in meditation.

The story is told of St. Francis Xavier, visiting a Buddhist monastery in Asia where he came upon a group of monks seated in meditation.

"What are those men doing?" he asked the abbot, noting the air of tranquillity that enveloped the meditation hall.

"Well," said the abbot, pointing each of them out in turn, "that one's thinking about what we're going to have for lunch today, and that one's wondering how he can get someone to offer him a smart new set of robes. That one's dreaming of the girl who came by yesterday and that one's planning how to get to the best houses when next we go on our alms round. . . ."

Such mental disturbances are pretty much inevitable when anyone sits down to meditate. You can't live your life thinking thoughts like these from moment to moment and then expect them to vanish just because you sit down and close your eyes.

The great Sri Lankan Buddhist commentator, Buddhaghosa, recounted a set of antidotes to distraction in meditation that can usefully be applied in cases like these.

To begin with, you become aware that you are in the grip of a mental hindrance. Then you recollect that you can do things in your meditation to deal with that hindrance.

First, you can work to cultivate the opposite state of mind to the hindrance you're experiencing. Second, you can consider the consequence of allowing the hindrance to continue unchecked. Third, you can cultivate a sky-like mind, seeing the hindrance as a temporary part of your experience rather like a cloud that arises in the sky and then just passes away. Fourth, you can grit your teeth and try to suppress the hindrance. And fifth, you can turn your mind to what is really most important to you—the desire to gain Enlightenment—and so return to your meditation with added vigor and commitment.

We can adapt these same methods to help us to deal with issues like craving in the context of our daily lives. For instance, we can use these five antidotes to help us deal with those compulsive spending urges that many of us experience from time to time, where we're driven to buy things we don't need, and perhaps don't even want, almost against our will.

TRY THIS:
FIVE ANTIDOTES TO COMPULSIVE SPENDING URGES
To begin with, we need to learn to spot compulsive spending urges for what they are, decide that we want to deal with them, and recognize that we're capable of doing so. After all, there are all kinds of ways in which we refrain from following our immediate desires: we don't punch people who annoy us, we don't steal things we like just because we can. Once we've seen that, we can begin to apply one or another antidote to our feelings of craving.

*Cultivate the Opposite*
Stop for a moment and reflect on how pleasant it would be not to be burdened with shopping urges. You could walk through town and look in shop windows and still be in charge of your own life (and wallet). You could read magazines for the articles and not be bothered by the ads. Your bank balance would be healthier and you could trade work for leisure more often. You could save your money and put it toward something you really care about—a great vacation with your family, or a friend or partner; or you could help a cause you really believe in. The opportunities to use your re-sources creatively are endless, but there you are, allowing them all to leak away. Rather than mindlessly giving mental energy to the desire to shop, we can give it to the desire *not* to shop mindlessly to be more directed in what we do with our energy.

Then, we can cultivate contentment by realizing that actually things are okay at base, just as they are, right now. Often we deliberately stimulate feelings of craving in ourselves because it gives us a sense of really "being someone." Maybe you've had this experience in an airport. The experience of being "processed" by the airline's necessary bureaucracy can be so dehumanizing. From the moment you check-in, it can seem that you're just another item in the airline's complex logistical operation. That's uncomfortable, so what you do is shop. Many airports have provided us with shopping malls in their departure lounges and so we can go off and reassert ourselves there. That way you get to express your potency to some extent—you're not an inert statistic, you're a person with the power of choice. Sometimes we fall into wanting things because that's a way of asserting ourselves in the world, of actually being someone.

But you never really stopped being someone in the first place. Just being yourself, doing what you're doing, being what you're being, is enough. Instead of going off to shop in the airport mall, you simply could have sat in a chair, quietly being yourself, observing the strange world all around you. That would do. You, as you now are, are the end product of billions of years of evolution. You've no need to own anything more to assert your identity and the way you flourish your credit card certainly doesn't add much to the sum total of your humanity.

The practice of meditation, which helps to give us a stronger experience of ourselves simply as we are, is a good way of cultivating "the opposite" of craving.

Another way of cultivating the opposite is by experiencing beauty without craving. Visit an art gallery, meet up with a friend and have a good conversation, go for a walk in a park or in the country. We can have access to beauty without buying it. Indeed, some of the most beautiful things we can experience—sunsets, great pictures, fine buildings, good conversation—we can never buy.

*Consider the Consequences of Allowing Your Craving to*
*Continue Unchecked*

It can help us to work with unskillful feelings if we think what
would happen to us if we let them just run on, unchecked. This becomes brutally obvious when we reflect on what would happen to
us if we never put a brake on our feelings of aversion, for example.
They might easily turn to hatred and, if that runs unchecked, turn
to the active desire to harm and that leads to the actual act of harming someone, even, in extreme cases, to murder. It doesn't get that
far with us because we don't let it.

But think about what would happen to your bank account if you
gave in to cravings at every turn—think about all of the other
things, things that really matter to you, that would be crowded out
of your life. And where are you going to put all this stuff you're
buying—don't you have enough clutter in your life? Think of the
hollow feeling you sometimes get when you've bought something
you thought would really make you happy and it doesn't really. Do
you want to have that feeling again?

*Cultivate a Sky-like Mind*

With this practice, you recognize that feelings such as craving arise
and pass away within your mind all the time and you actually don't
have to act on any of them. With an interested attention, you can
watch them arising and passing away, like clouds in the sky. You can
simply attend to the feeling, seeing where it comes from, noting
how it is now, and reflecting that it won't be around for very much
longer. It is, after all, just a feeling. This practice requires us to identify ourselves not only with our immediate feelings but also with
the mental space around them, the space of our overall experience,
which is bigger than our feelings and which contains them. Again,
the practice of meditation is very good for helping to bring such an
experience about.

## Suppression

If none of these first three methods work, you can just say no. Grit your teeth, use your will power, wait for the shopping urge to pass and don't give in. You know you can do this. Many of us, for example, are prone to be irritated by other people from time to time. But when we are, we don't lash out at them with our tongue, let alone our fists, because we've been schooled not to. We've learned to suppress our desire to harm others because it's antisocial. Things like shopping urges seem more innocent, and our society doesn't disapprove of them so strongly, so we tend to go along with them. But just as, from time to time, we suppress our tendency to be angry with others, so we can suppress our tendency to want to buy.

This kind of suppression is not the same as repression. In the latter we deny even to ourselves that we feel unacceptable feelings like anger or sexual desire, and that can lead to strange distortions in our behavior. In the case of suppression, however, we're fully aware of what it is that we feel, we just don't act upon it.

Even though this can be a bit painful at first, once you've achieved a few successes in this way it becomes very much easier.

## Make a Commitment

In the end you can only apply these methods if you have decided that you really do want to change your behavior in a certain way. It is important to think about the values you hold. What sort of person do you want to be? Write a list of the qualities that you'd like to have more fully than you do at present. When you are clear about this, commit yourself to your highest values and try always to bear them in mind. Turn them over in your mind. Try to make a habit of reflecting on them for a few moments at least once a day.

We don't work to overcome our reactive desires because they're bad in themselves. Rather, we do so because we want to make room for our more creative desires to flourish, and our more creative desires are often tied, not to material possessions, but to somewhat more intangible matters—to our relationships, for example, with friends and family, to our personal development and to causes we really believe in. A clue to where our creative desires lie is to consider the direction in which our voluntary generosity tends to flow: that which we give to is that which we really care about, and when we give, as we saw, we build up our stock of hidden wealth.

But we have hidden wealth in other areas too. Above all, our hidden wealth is our capacity for happiness.

Once, a king came to the Buddha to ask him about his teaching, and in the course of the discussion the question arose: which of them was the happier—the Buddha or the king? The king was quite sure that he was the happier by far of the two.

"I've got all these palaces," he said. "I've got an army and all this wealth—to say nothing of my beautiful wives. It's pretty clear that I'm happier than you. What have you got? Here you are sitting underneath a tree outside some wretched hut. You've got a yellow robe and a measly begging bowl. That's all. So obviously, I'm by far the happier of the two."

"All right," the Buddha said, "let's discuss it. Let me put you a question. Could you sit here perfectly still for an hour, enjoying complete and perfect happiness?"

"Yes, I suppose I could," the king replied.

"That's well and good," the Buddha said. "But could you sit here without moving, enjoying complete and perfect happiness, for six hours?"

"Hmm . . . that would be rather difficult," said the king.

"And could you sit here for a whole day and a whole night, without moving, absolutely happy the whole time?" the Buddha asked.

"No, that would be beyond me," the king admitted.

"Well, I can tell you this," the Buddha said. "I can sit here for seven days and seven nights, without moving, without stirring, and all that time experience complete and perfect happiness without any change, without any diminution whatsoever. So," he said, "I think I am happier than you are."

The Buddha's hidden wealth, his contentment and his capacity for happiness, was far beyond the wealth of any king.

In our own more limited experience, our ability to take delight in nature, in other people, in the arts, the sciences and culture, in our work and in our friendships—all of these are aspects of our hidden wealth, and we trade them for tangible wealth very often at a cost to ourselves. You work more so you see less of your kids and you never have the time to go out into the mountains the way you used to. Even when you have time off, too often you spend it just recovering.

The trouble with hidden wealth is that mostly it remains just that—hidden—and so we can sacrifice it without really being aware of what we're doing. In order to avoid that, we've got to become more conscious of our hidden wealth, and of its value to us. What are the things that really matter to you? What is their order of priority in your life? How much would it take for you to sacrifice them?

TRY THIS:

List the ten most significant things you've acquired or done in the past three years. By significant, we don't only mean the things you spent lots of money on, though you should include those, we also mean the things that have been important to you and made a difference to your life. Continue with this exercise as demonstrated by Katie's example below.

Katie, who lives near Palo Alto, thought about the things that had happened in the past three years. The family had bought a new car, a new freezer and redecorated the house. They had taken a trip to France and another to Yosemite. They'd picked up a pet dog, a Skye terrier called Talisker, from the pound. She'd taken a course in meditation at her local Buddhist center and also begun regularly to attend yoga classes. Her son, John, had graduated from college and she'd been on a Buddhist retreat.

Placing these in order of cost, John's college tuition topped the lot. Then there was the car, the trip to France and the redecoration. Taken over three years, her yoga classes came next, then the freezer, the trip to Yosemite and the retreat. The meditation course cost very little and Talisker was pretty much free.

Ranking them from one to ten, where one was the lowest cost and ten the highest, they looked like this:

1. Talisker
2. Meditation course
3. New freezer
4. Retreat
5. Yosemite
6. Yoga classes
7. Redecoration
8. Trip to France
9. New car
10. John's college tuition

Ranking them in order of value was much harder, but after a great deal of crossing out and soul-searching, it came out as follows:

John's college tuition was up on top in terms of value. No one would argue with that. But what came next? Talisker was really a member of the family now and Katie couldn't imagine giving him up for any amount of money. Then it had to be either the meditation course or the retreat. Both of them had really changed her life. Perhaps the course would have to come first, because without it she'd not have gone on the retreat. Then there was her yoga. It really helped to keep her sane and healthy. The trip to Yosemite was really wonderful—their last vacation as a family—and France, after that, was a bit of a washout really, maybe it had better go last. The redecoration made a difference to her. They had to have a freezer, but was it more important to her than the car? No, perhaps not. . . . So when it came to the order of value, from one to ten, where one is a low value, it looked like this:

1. Trip to France
2. New freezer
3. New car
4. Redecoration
5. Vacation in Yosemite
6. Yoga
7. Retreat
8. Meditation course
9. Talisker
10. John's college tuition

We can now take Katie's two lists and graph them on a chart which relates costs to value (see next page). As you'll see, there is a diagonal line that runs up the chart from the bottom left-hand corner. Things found to the left of this line represent particularly good value, while those to the right give little satisfaction in relation to their cost. Does this mean that Katie ought to sell the family car and buy a whole breeding pack of Skye terriers with the proceeds? Probably not. Part of Talisker's value, after all, lies in his uniqueness. But it does mean that projects like holidays in France should be carefully considered in the future, and Katie should think very carefully, when the car is due for replacement, about whether she really needs to buy new or if a used one would do.

Now we can give the exercise another twist. We can ask you, and Katie, to list the ten things in life that are most important to you at the moment, and cost them.

Right away Katie thought about her husband Fred and her son John, her mom and dad, and her best friend, Jane. She thought about John's graduation, her job and some of the people at work. Her neighbors and Talisker . . .

"Wait a minute," said Katie, "I can't do that. There are far too many of them. I could never rank them, let alone cost them!"

And that's just the point. For that is Katie's hidden wealth. Its value is infinite and its economic costs are low. But by practicing

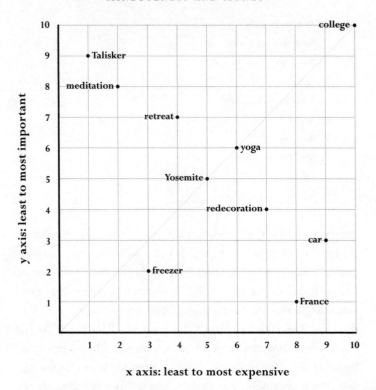

**x axis: least to most expensive**

contentment you'll find you're able to acknowledge and extend it. (Talisker, of course, still thinks that he tops the list any day.)

List your hidden wealth. Write down why the items on the list are valuable to you.

## Relating to Actual Wealth: Holding Loosely

If we are confident in the state of our hidden wealth, if the friendships and other relationships that mean most to us are in good repair, if our capacity to be happy—to delight in the simple things in life—has been developed, then our relationship to tangible wealth will be healthier.

Norman Fischer, the Zen teacher, poet and former abbot of the San Francisco Zen Center, tells the following story.

"I was talking to a friend recently and I said 'How are you doing?' 'I'm miserable,' he replied. 'Why are you miserable?' I asked. 'I just lost half my money.' 'Wow,' I said, 'how did that happen?' And it seems that he had a certain amount of money, he put it into some investment, the numbers on paper increased to a certain extent and then decreased. But nothing else happened. Literally, nothing else happened to him—the numbers went up, then they came down—and my friend was first of all elated and then he was miserable. But nothing else changed. He still lived in the same house, ate the same food, wore the same clothes. . . . Everything was the same as before. But he had gone from elation and a feeling of tremendous wealth to a feeling of poverty. Of course those numbers had meaning for my friend, they represented a disappointing reality, but what he didn't see was that that was just one take on reality. From another perspective nothing meaningful had changed and there really was nothing to be upset about."

Of course, we're not all in a position where losses, in the stock market or in other investments, are only a matter of numbers changing. For some of us such reversals will deal a significant blow to our dreams of freedom and independence. Such losses can cause pain and anguish. We feel we've been somehow diminished by them, and certainly many of us sometimes have to change our plans as our retirement nest egg isn't so certain and we're going to have to work longer and harder to put our children through college.

Not all losses, however, impact on how we actually live and it's important to put things in perspective. So, reflect. If you've taken a loss on the markets in the past few years, how much does it really matter? Is it a real loss, one that will actually affect how you live, or is it a paper loss that makes no tangible difference to your life, apart from how you feel about yourself?

But what *about* real losses? What if you're going to have postpone your retirement, carry a larger burden of debt or ask your child to choose a cheaper college?

Kulananda's father spent most of his working life in South Africa until, after multiple bypass surgery, he took early retirement from a stress-filled job. Fulfilling a lifetime's ambition, Kulananda's parents emigrated to Israel, where his father started a business.

A year later Israel became involved in a war in Lebanon and inflation skyrocketed to an unprecedented rate of 20 percent per month. Kulananda's father was forced to sell out and take a salaried position. Then, the South African currency began a steep decline, and the South African pension on which his parents had largely relied on to continue their previous standard of living fell to a tenth of what it had been when they left that country.

How have Kulananda's parents reacted to these reversals? At first, they were dismayed. They'd expected to live out their lives at a particular standard of living which was no longer in reach, and Kulananda's father had to carry on his working life for longer than he'd planned. These were painful realizations. But, Kulananda noted, one adjusts, and he's been impressed by his parents' resilience. They very quickly learned the importance of leaving the past behind and dealing creatively with the situation they now found themselves faced with.

With the computer the family bought him for his seventieth birthday, his father started a website selling mattresses on the Internet, and that has helped to offset his drop in income, to a small extent. He also started a small garden on their apartment terrace and, his parents say, they get as much or more pleasure from that as they did from their large South African garden. His father has started to meditate and says that this helps him to weather the many ups and downs of living and working in Israel today. Adapting one of the parables of the Buddha, he says that he regards his old life in South Africa as a raft. Without it they could not have got where they are now, but that life having served its purpose in getting them where they now are, they have no problem with having left it behind. They enjoy their current life even more than they did when they were well-off financially.

Needless to say, we live in a consumerist culture and many of us have dependents. It's very well to speak of the need to foster more contentment and to live a simpler life ourselves, but what about those who depend on us? Can we make those same decisions for them? We may learn something here by turning again to Norman Fischer and seeing how he went about things. Although we may not all be in a position to emulate Norman's approach, we can learn from how he dealt with this question in his own life.

For much of his adult life, Norman lived with his wife and two sons at Green Gulch Farm, a monastery associated with the San Francisco Zen Center, in Marin County just north of San Francisco. What was it like bringing up his two boys on a small monastic stipend in one of the wealthiest parts of the world?

"When they were in middle school, about thirteen to fifteen years old, there was a time when they were very embarrassed by our way of life. I remember they'd have me drop them off at school some blocks away, so that people wouldn't see our beat-up old car—or my shaved head! It wasn't as if they were eating themselves up alive, they were just embarrassed at the comparison between their own economics and that of their friends."

By then Norman's wife, Kathie, was teaching school and living at Green Gulch was fairly inexpensive, so they had some disposable income.

"Our kids didn't go to school looking scandalously ragged or anything like that. They didn't have the highest of the high brand-name sneakers or whatever, but it was within reason."

When the boys went to high school, however, they got scholarships to one of the most exclusive private high schools in San Francisco.

"Now they were going to school with these extremely wealthy people, and they also had more confidence, they'd grown up a bit more, and they were very proud of, and positive about, the distinction between themselves and these other people. They were proud of the fact that they were from Green Gulch, it was a source of interest—something unique about them. I don't know what their friends thought, but to the boys it was cool. They'd tell people about it all the time, and invite their friends to our house. We lived in an unbelievably tiny, falling-down room. It had been a cattle pen that was remade into a little house, and I guess they felt proud of that too in a way.

"They also began to have deeper social concerns. They felt that ethically and politically our simple way of life was more righteous and true than the life of those fabulously wealthy people. They noticed that their contemporaries were confused and troubled by wealth. Sometimes their friends knew that, at other times they didn't seem to, but my sons could see it. So they ended up feeling really positive about our way of life.

"There were two sides to our life—the economic, which you could view as a life of deprivation—and the spiritual; and the economic deprivation was way outweighed by the moral and spiritual riches we had. I think they perfectly understood that those two seemed to be connected somehow. By the time they were in high school they really had it figured out. They'd developed a strong sense of values which they have to this day, and I think they will continue to have."

Partly aided by scholarships again, Norman's son Aron went to Harvard and Noah to the Rhode Island School of Design.

"They're practically minded people, so they think about how they're going to make a livelihood, of course, but they're far more concerned with aesthetic and spiritual and ethical values. That's their focus, which I think is wonderful."

Did Norman have any anxieties as the boys were growing up about how he'd be able to fund their education?

"No, because I knew the implications of the life that I'd chosen. I knew that I'd chosen a life in which I could expect nothing for myself or my children. I knew that that was what I was doing, and I thought, well, that's the way it is. Whatever happens is going to happen and I'll trust reality to provide what it needs, and whatever difficulties we have, we'll have to turn them into character-building advantages, there's no choice."

Of course not everyone's kids are going to receive scholarships. But that's not the point of this story. If you decide to simplify your life, one of the consequences will be that you will have more time to spend with your family. That means more time to help your children to develop a set of values that will enable them to get through life in a healthy, human way. No amount of money can buy that, and no amount can compensate for its lack.

When he speaks of how things have turned out for him and his family, Norman attributes much of their good fortune to luck. Perhaps he's being unduly modest there. One could also attribute it to the positive results that inevitably follow from a life skillfully lived.

# SEVEN

# The fourth Precept:
# Be Honest

*Don't lie, cultivate truthfulness.*

## Truthfulness

Not many of our readers are going to perpetrate fraud on a large scale, but how many of these statements have that little ring of familiarity for you?

"I'm sure I sent that check off last week. It must have gotten lost somehow. I'll get one off tomorrow."

("Darn! I thought I'd have a least three more weeks on that one. Now, how much was it for?")

"Honey, I'd love us to re-do the kitchen, but the way things are going at work right now I just don't think we can afford it."

("You might want a new kitchen, but I've been thinking about a new car.")

"Of course I only use the car for business purposes. It's a genuine taxable expense. When you're working for yourself you don't have that much time for socializing!"

("If you can't get this one past the IRS I'm getting myself a new accountant.")

When we speak like this, we take ourselves off for another spin around the Wheel, and keep ourselves locked in states of narrow self-confinement. We may like to think that a little untruth never hurt anyone, but it does—it hurts us, by keeping us confined in states of constricted self-concern, and it hurts others, by perpetuating the smog of delusion.

The deliberate pursuit of truthfulness, on the other hand, clears the air around us. It leaves us better off as we can see more clearly where we stand and where we're going. When we're honest, people feel they can trust us and that makes our dealings with them much more straightforward. We know ourselves and what we really want, and others know us to be ourselves—they know that what you see is what you get. The ability to trust people in that way is the foundation of all economic transactions.

Vajraketu, the CEO of Windhorse Trading, the Buddhist company that Kulananda founded, knows that he can call up their bank anytime and ask for an extra $200,000 on their overdraft. All he has to do is to explain the circumstances. "It's no problem," the manager has said. "We know we can trust you."

"Is this a good seller?" trade customers often ask the salespeople at Windhorse Trading, and sometimes they'll be surprised when the answer comes back "No, not really." They can also sometimes be surprised when placing an order to have it suggested that perhaps they're buying too much of a product and that it might be better to start with a smaller amount and see how they get on.

They used to light the glass products in their own retail shops with bright halogen spotlights. It made them look great. But then they considered that their customers were unlikely to do the same at home. It didn't seem right to allow their customers to buy a product which would look quite different when they got it home, so they changed the lighting to something that approximates more closely to the lighting found in ordinary homes.

Truthfulness in financial relations builds trust and is the only basis upon which the kind of mutual respect that is essential in any creative relationship can grow.

As well as refraining from the good old-fashioned outright lie, we should strive to be accurate and straightforward in our dealings with others. That means not exaggerating things to gain an advantage, and not minimizing them either. This isn't always easy. That old car you want to sell—what will you say when a potential buyer asks how many times it's broken down in the past year? If you're not honest about how many times it's broken down, your lack of straightforwardness will affect you in other ways. It will admit more vagueness and unclarity into your life and lead you away from the Path of Abundance and into a narrower world of defensive self-concern.

It will also reinforce your ability to fudge the truth in future situations so that the next time the truth seems a little uncomfortable, it'll be easier to lie. Behave like that enough, and people start to feel that they can't altogether trust you and that strengthens the barrier between yourself and others.

Our apparently innocent avoidances of the truth have much bigger consequences than we might first think, because when it comes to the law of karma, there's no such thing as a free lunch. All our voluntary acts of body, speech and mind have their effects in terms of who we are and what we next become. "Well," you may say, "it's a fairly innocent little lie. After all, no one altogether expects people selling used cars to be totally honest with them. . . ." But when we speak untruths we just add another puff of smoke to the fog of delusion in which we're all stumbling about and no one gains from that.

"If you speak delusions, everything becomes a delusion," wrote Ryokan, the eighteenth-century hermit, poet and Zen master.

> *If you speak the truth, everything becomes the truth.*
> *Outside the truth there is no delusion,*

*But outside delusion there is no special truth.*
*Followers of the Buddha's Way!*
*Why do you earnestly seek the truth in distant places?*
*Look for delusion and truth in the bottom of your own hearts.*[18]

TRY THIS:
Reflect. In the past twenty-four hours, did you tell any lies for the sake of gain or to avoid loss or just to have your own way? Or did you try to hide the truth behind a wall of vagueness? What were the consequences for you? What might have happened if you'd been more honest? Can you avoid that kind of behavior in the future? What changes to your life would you need to make to avoid repeating that kind of behavior in the future?

## Authenticity

The deepest challenge, when it comes to speaking the truth, is simply to be fully and authentically ourselves, in all situations. That isn't easy, and for many of us it is most acutely difficult in the context of the workplace. In our leisure time we can choose to associate with family and friends who share our values and beliefs, or at least who'll make an effort to understand us. At work, most of us are forced into association with people, some of whom are not that sympathetic to what we most deeply believe. This isn't always easy, and for some of the people we've spoken to, the quest for truthfulness at work has meant that they've had to make significant changes to their careers.

Matthew Webb joined the investment bank JP Morgan at the age of twenty-two, having graduated with a degree in economics from Cambridge University.

---

18. Trans. John Stevens, *One Robe, One Bowl: The Zen Poetry of Ryokan* (New York and Tokyo: Weatherhill, 1996).

"It seemed the natural culmination of the way my life was going at the time. I'd had an easy, privileged childhood. I just assumed I'd be able to make lots of money at some point and I had no idea what else to do with myself. So when I was offered the job I decided to give it a chance."

He began to work as a bond salesman. By talking on the phone for eleven hours a day, buying and selling other people's money, a tiny but significant percentage of it would appear in his bank account at the end of the month. That was nice, and by the time he was twenty-three he started to be quite successful. He got to do some of the bigger trades and began to enjoy the glamour that goes with the world of finance at that level—business-class travel, limousines and expensive restaurants. For about a year and half it was really exciting. He got pay raises every six months and an annual bonus. Yes, he worked eleven- or twelve-hour days, but what else was there to do?

Deep down, however, Matthew knew that his heart wasn't really in that kind of business. He wanted to be a success, and appear to be so, but he found he couldn't put himself heart and soul into bond trading.

"It was all so dull and repetitive—telephone sales with large numbers and the odd nice lunch."

"Is this what I want to do with my life?" he asked himself. It seemed plain to him that most of his peers were dissatisfied as well, but none of them were talking about it.

"I certainly didn't want to open myself up and share what I really cared about in that environment. It was a shark pool, and I knew that if I opened my heart up there it would be squashed. People could be treated so callously. If you were laid off, you never even had the chance to return to your desk to fetch your jacket—you were just out the door and that was that."

The big marker of success, though, was money and Matthew began to earn larger and larger amounts of it. He also learned to play the game. When he received his first large bonus, for example, he knew that he should keep a poker face and not show his boss, whom he got on quite well with, that he was pleased. "What's up, Matt?" his boss asked. "Are you all right with that? I thought it's what you wanted?" But Matthew played it cool. "It's okay," he said and, when he left that evening, he danced down the street whooping for joy.

Matthew saved his money, avoiding the extravagant lifestyle of his colleagues.

"I had a constant sense that I might want to leave there at a moment's notice and I needed to be able to do that. I never bought more than one month's ticket for public transportion at a time, for example, even though it cost more to travel that way. I knew that life wasn't going to be for me forever and I didn't want to leave there with nothing but gray hair and heart disease."

When traveling in Kathmandu before joining the bank, Matthew had encountered Buddhism and learned to meditate. On his return, he began to attend classes at the London Buddhist Centre. His involvement with the Centre was rather sporadic at first, but he kept a regular meditation practice going and felt that the Centre was a handhold in another world that he didn't want to let go of. Gradually the meditation started to have more of an effect. After sitting in the morning he'd arrive at work feeling purposeful and clear, but over the course of the day he'd feel his calm unraveling under the pressures of work.

Eventually he went on a Buddhist retreat and found that he enjoyed the consistently positive states he was able to reach in those conditions. It was so good to sustain a positive state of mind and not have it crumble as the day went on. He decided to quit his job and take up a position with the Karuna Trust, working with other Buddhists to help raise money to fund social and educational projects in India.

"People were really surprised at work. I was just starting to earn really big money after all. 'Don't you realize you could be making a million dollars a year in a few years time?' they asked. 'Do you have family money or something?' "

He became something of a curiosity in the office. People he hardly knew came over to see if they could discover what it was all about. Here was a guy who could stay and make lots of money but he was leaving—voluntarily. What was he up to?

"On the face of it they thought we had everything—health, status, intelligence, money—but many of them knew there was something about it that wasn't quite right. That's why I was suddenly so interesting. 'What's he found that he could just give this all up?' But I couldn't answer. I couldn't tell them that I was following this tiny speck of light that I'd found—I wasn't even sure about it myself— how could I reveal that part of my life in the atmosphere of skepticism and cynicism that there was in the bank?"

Now working for Karuna, Matthew earns around 10 percent of what he did before. Much of his work involves going around to people's houses in the evenings, knocking on their doors and asking them if they'd be willing to become supporters of the work in India.

"I see into so many people's lives, and it's especially interesting to see into the lives of those whom I'd have become. I can sense the restrictions they live with, the work they have to do, the daily stresses they have to face. And what for? I was in a lovely house recently, one I'd have liked myself. 'Nice house,' I told the guy. 'Well, the bank owns most of it,' he said."

What Matthew has at Karuna is work he loves doing in a context in which he can fully be himself.

"It makes me bigger, not smaller. I feel so much more alive, being aware and trying to communicate empathetically with people on their doorsteps. This is work that I actually want to do, it's not something that I have to do in order to be able to do something else. I love the engagement with other idealistic people, working from heartfelt motives. Now my life and work aren't separate anymore. I'm not selling my time, giving up eleven hours each day so that I'll have time for other things at some point in the future. And it's not a contract anymore. It's more a relationship of free, mutual giving. I give to my workmates, to the Trust and to our donors and they all give to me."

The fact that his work is now based in the practice of generosity is important to Matthew, but it's not the most essential thing.

"I want to connect with other people and to feel alive. People are the most interesting things there are. If others are real and being themselves, then in communication with them I feel real too. In fund-raising I try to allow others just to be themselves, to be genuine. That's what allows the gem of generosity to emerge, and that's what I really care about."

Cheryl Manzano found her dream job after graduate school in a leading market research firm. She found the work, and the people she worked with, immensely stimulating. They were bright, vivacious, challenging people, intent on bringing new perspectives on the world of business. On one project, for example, they set out to create new opportunities for a troubled part of the U.S. textile industry. It was a fantastically ambitious and exciting project that would lead to many changes. Many of the businesses they were working with at that time were protected by U.S. tariff legislation that priced out imports. With the opening up of America to international trade it was no longer possible to maintain that. How could the restructuring be done in a way that enabled the U.S. businesses to survive? Some jobs would have to go in the restructuring, but restructuring is like surgery: you try to save the patient before it's too late. One of the senior people working for a client painted a gloomy picture of what would happen if the project failed. "Broadly speaking, the problem for us is ensuring that our mills don't end up as folk museums." The project worked: the market opportunities that they found created new kinds of jobs and made a big difference to many people's lives.

Being able to make that kind of difference gave Cheryl a real sense of potency and effectiveness.

There was tremendous emphasis on integrity in her firm, on the importance of truth and finding it out; and they took extraordinary pains never to let anyone down. And it was on a point of personal integrity that Cheryl eventually felt that she had to leave. More specifically, it was because she was in love, and the person she was in love with was in New York and she was finding it harder and harder to get away from her assignments in the Southeast. The issue was partly one of time. Long working weeks were not uncommon. But another factor was her sexual identity. The person she was in love with was another woman, and at the time, Cheryl felt, possibly incorrectly, that she couldn't be "out" in her work environment. She started telling lies about why she had to go back to New York almost every weekend.

One day, Jo, her boss, for whom she had tremendous respect, said: "Tell me, all these trips to New York . . . it's got to be a hot new boyfriend."

"He's really sweet," Cheryl replied.

"I'm so pleased for you!" Jo said. "We're going to be in New York too this weekend. My husband and I would just love it if you guys joined us for a show."

And that was the cue for Cheryl to make other plans: in fact, to quit a job she really loved. She couldn't bear to be so inauthentic. She left the market research firm and took a job with one of the firm's clients in New York. Sadly, her relationship ended not long afterward. Her girlfriend had found Cheryl's lack of authenticity hard to bear as well. The story doesn't quite end there, however. Cheryl never completely lost contact with her old boss, and came clean to her a few years later. They are friends now, and Jo has given Cheryl help and encouragement in the subsequent stages of her career.

In order to feel that they were being fully themselves at work, both Matthew and Cheryl had to change their jobs. Vijayamala made the ability to be fully herself a condition of her taking on a new job in the first place.

A certified public accountant who now runs the accounts department at Windhorse Trading, Vijayamala started meditating at nineteen, while she was studying for a degree in psychology. After graduating, she wasn't clear what to do with her life. She wanted to make a difference, but how? Since she also wanted to travel for a while, she decided to visit India and see if she could contribute in some way to the work being done there by members of the Western Buddhist Order.

It soon became clear that the Karuna Trust needed someone to serve as a communications link between the British donors and the local Indian project workers. Vijayamala had a job.

She spent a few months at the Karuna offices in London, where she saw that one of the things that most clearly needed to be communicated between donors and project workers was financial information. Donors needed to feel that their money was being spent wisely. Project workers needed to understand the donors' needs and perceptions. She started to learn about accounts, did a few short accounting courses, and discovered that she could do that kind of work well.

"In those days the people I was working with all felt that they wanted to change the world for the better, but in a way we had nothing but our goodwill. That was something, but it wasn't enough. We had a vision of how things could be, but we lacked the professional skills needed to put that into practice."

After working in India for a time she decided to return to England and qualify as an accountant.

"I come from a highly academic family. Almost every single one of my family members teaches in some kind of way. So the engagement with business that came along with the accounting training felt like a real adventure to me. It was a great challenge. But Buddhism isn't a kind of escapism. It has to go out and meet the world. By entering the financial world, my personal quest to find a task in life came face-to-face with a simple objective need—if we were going to make a difference to things, Buddhists needed to be skilled."

During the period of her training, Vijayamala kept up her meditation practice, found time for retreats and stayed in contact with her spiritual friends.

"It was really important to me then to keep those links up. It helped to keep my vision alive while I was doing the training. Accounting offices aren't always inspiring places to be!"

Once she qualified, Vijayamala was approached by the directors of Windhorse Trading and offered a job. She agreed to join them, provided she could set up an all-female accounts team.

"I wanted to lead a full-on Buddhist life, where work was fully incorporated into my spiritual life. In my experience life is so much simpler when sexual tensions don't get in the way of other things. I've always found I can go deeper into things with other people in a single-sex context. I didn't want to work in a place where you spend eight hours a day working and then go home and get on with your real life. I was looking for the kind of continuity of relationship with others that, outside of family life, you usually only find in traditional societies. In our team we try to share *all* aspects of our lives together. As well as working together, many of us live communally in different groupings with one another, so we get very involved in the details of each other's lives. From my experience, it is more straightforward to do this in a single-sex context. It reduces some of the subtle, and often not so subtle, need-based relating, that can happen at that level of intimacy in mixed-sex situations."

In traditional societies women have taken a mainly supportive role. For Vijayamala, it's important for women to take initiative and achieve success, but without losing their sense of connectedness with others.

"Too often these days we see successful women having to sacrifice a lot for their careers and ending up in states of emotional isolation and loneliness. In our team, we want to achieve the same success, but without that emotional cost."

She wanted to help establish a working situation that allowed people to go beyond the idea of a "role" in the first place, for what is a role apart from an aspect of ego-identity that Buddhists try to transcend?

"This is something really valuable that Buddhism has to offer us today and I wanted to bring that into our work. Women today seem to find themselves quite torn. You can have the role of a successful career woman, or the role of a wife, mother or family member. A lot of juggling goes on. This role or that role. I want to make a kind of 'role-free zone' at work, where people are simply themselves, doing whatever needs to be done, and we bend to fit in with each other's needs. We encourage each other in the work, talk to each other about the direction of our lives, support each other in times of family crisis—simply relating in the way that is most appropriate at any given moment.

"I want to be an independent woman, who can hold her own in what is still, to some extent, a man's world, without sacrificing the qualities of empathetic relationship that are often ascribed to the traditional role of women. The chance to work in a women's team, and one that places such a strong emphasis on independence and success *as well as* on friendship, empathy and communication is really rare, and incredibly valuable."

Jim Conroy's experience of the corporate world is somewhat different from Matthew Webb's. He works for eBA, British Airways' new web-based department, as a project manager for a team that is developing solutions for British Airways' agents and customers. Jim loves his work.

"It's the best place I've ever worked in. The people are positive and clever. It's a no-blame culture where we just get on and fix things. You can see the results of all your work unfolding before your eyes. I really like the way in which everyone treats each other with respect. There's no hierarchy; the management team is accessible and doesn't rely on status."

Jim is a trustee of his local Buddhist center where he also

teaches one evening each week. His work, he says, and the center's classes are two aspects of the same thing. In fact, it was due to Buddhism that he began his career in IT.

"My first real break came when I got my original position at British Airways, back in 1988. A close Buddhist friend of mine was working there himself and told me that they needed someone with training skills and a computer science background. I'd been working for some months in the Buddhist center but I could see that it wasn't right for me—I decided to make the move."

His Buddhist practice has also had a deeper influence.

"I'd been interested in Buddhism for some time. But I didn't get really committed to it until my best friend was killed in a road accident when we were in our early twenties. I found the Buddhist center so supportive, and the Buddhist teachings about impermanence helped me to reach some level of understanding and acceptance about what had happened."

The experience also taught him that life is extraordinarily precious, uncertain and not to be wasted.

"You spend so much of your life at work. For me, Buddhism is constantly raising questions about the worth of what I'm doing. Am I wasting my time here? Is this really what I want to do? Am I in a place where I can really make a difference?"

For Jim, work in the corporate world involves a constant challenge to be true to himself—and to practice the precepts.

"Even at eBA, there's a certain amount of negative gossip that's easy to get drawn into, but if you stay aware, there's always the chance to affect the conversational flow in a positive way. There are many, many small decision points—to be authentic or let myself down—in the course of every day. I try to get it right. My performance appraisals don't log the fact that I'm a Buddhist—although it's generally known—but I get great feedback about the effect that I'm having on others, and I appreciate that."

Much of Jim's job is about ensuring very clear communication—bringing people together and clarifying expectations.

"My Buddhist training helps me to get behind the undercurrents and emotional aspects at play. My job is to uncover what's been hidden, to look for what people on my team have not said, whose eyes won't meet someone else's. To do that, I need to be very aware of how I am too.

"I've probably described eBA at its best. There are issues for me about the balance of work and life, which is difficult to manage, particularly because I enjoy my job so much. It's a demanding job and there are moments when I get tired and emotionally distant. I'd like to have more time for my partner and my friends. And, great as the eBA environment might be, Enlightenment is not the business's objective. The challenge is to learn how to live so that my Buddhist practice and my work reinforce each other. I feel that's happening more and more."

The kind of authenticity that Matthew, Cheryl and Vijayamala are all seeking in their working lives finds its culmination, perhaps, in the example of Norman Fischer, who was paid, for a time, simply to be himself and for no other purpose.

After nearly thirty years of being associated with the San Francisco Zen Center, Norman decided it was time for a change, and he left the center, setting up the Everyday Zen Foundation because, he thought, it was time to experiment with everyday American life.

The transition from living in a secure monastic context to getting by on whatever donations came in was eased somewhat by a large donation made to Everyday Zen by an old friend of his, Mel Ziegler.

Mel, who with his wife Patricia founded the clothing store chain Banana Republic and later helped to found the Republic of Tea, was in the process of establishing a new company, ZoZa, that was going to sell "Zen-inspired" clothing on the Web. He asked Norman to write a few short pieces for his website and Norman was happy to do that. Mel offered to pay for them, but Norman suggested he just make a donation to Everyday Zen. Later, Mel asked his friend to be the company's Zen advisor, their Zen abbot.

"But what could I possibly do for you?" Norman asked. "Nothing," Mel replied. "What this company needs, is nothing! We're all so busy running around that it would be nice to have somebody around who was on our team who wasn't really concerned with any of that but just provided an open window." Norman wouldn't have agreed to such a proposal under any other circumstances but Mel was an old friend whom he'd known for many years, and they had always kept up a dialogue about spiritual matters, so he agreed to do it.

From Mel's perspective, Norman made a real difference. "He was really wonderful. The work was really exciting but very stressful. Out of nothing there was suddenly 10,000 square feet of offices full of people who didn't know each other, furiously trying to create clothing, a website, a business structure—designing clothes, designing the website. Norman would come in occasionally and just by his very presence people would gather together and talk. He came in and conducted a service when one of the partners died. But he didn't really *do* anything. He just hung out, and he brought with him his unique perspective, which is very genuine and true. The thing about Norman . . . he's the Zen abbot who could be running an auto parts store. He really could, he's so unpretentious. He's just there, in a genuinely humble, awake and compassionate way. There's nothing more—no other agenda. He's so much the real thing in a world full of celebrities and people who just act out different roles. It's really refreshing, and he has the effect of drawing the same thing out of other people. He's so accessible that people were happy to just be with him and talk to him."

TRY THIS:

Reflect. How authentic are you able to be in your workplace? Are there things at work you can change in order to allow yourself to be more authentic? If you really can't be yourself, is it worth keeping that job?

## Right Speech

From a Buddhist perspective, the ethical dimension of how we communicate doesn't stop at telling the truth. According to the Buddha there is both right and wrong speech. Right speech is usually described as speech which is truthful, kindly or affectionate, helpful and productive of concord, harmony and unity. Wrong speech is untruthful, harsh, harmful and promotes discord, disharmony and disunity.

Ronna Kabatznick, Ph.D., a practicing Buddhist and psychologist, is a principal at MGH Consulting, a management consulting firm in Oakland, California. She uses the framework of right speech when working with executives and business teams, helping them to develop trust and improve communication skills in the workplace.

"So much suffering in the workplace—in fact everywhere—has to do with wrong speech. So if I work with a team, and they're trying to develop trust, one of the things that we talk about is speaking only what's truthful; not gossiping; speaking humbly, not arrogantly; and speaking only what's useful, rather than just for the sake of hearing yourself speak—which is something a lot of businesspeople really enjoy!"

Ronna encourages the teams she works with to adopt these guidelines as standards for what they call "team speech." Because it can be so difficult to maintain these standards in their communication with one another, Ronna asks them to make a private agreement with themselves and a public agreement with each other. Everyone signs the guidelines, as a way of demonstrating their commitment to this process. It may seem silly, but it works. Then she teaches them ways in which they can, as a team, help one another to practice right speech throughout the day. The whole team takes responsibility for seeing that the standard is maintained.

"If somebody's gossiping, for example, someone else in the

team can point that out, 'That isn't our team speech.' They can raise their awareness by asking, 'Are you aware this is not our team speech?' They can also indicate the impact wrong speech has: 'The way you're talking, which isn't team speech, makes me uncomfortable.' "

Ronna has executives practicing this kind of thing with each other, working to bring a higher level of awareness to their speech at all times.

"It's not easy to be mindful of one's speech. The Buddha said it's one of the most challenging mindfulness practices. People really have to work at it. Gossip, for instance, is so seductive, it's really easy to start doing it without thinking. You forget. Or you fall into harsh speech, ten minutes after you've agreed to avoid it. Before you know it, you're bad-mouthing someone and calling him or her a jerk. When you're reminded, 'Hey, that's not team speech,' it's like waking up. 'Oh! . . . yeah, you're right. What was I thinking?' "

The teams that follow and reinforce the right-speech guideline experience radical changes in their relationships. They report higher levels of trust, productivity and camaraderie. They also recount that there's much more time in the day since people aren't gossiping, bragging, complaining or calling unnecessary attention to themselves.

"That's the main thing that people notice. When you're not engaging in wrong speech, there's very little to say. You have to be more imaginative when you're working with Right Speech. Compliment instead of criticize; speak kindly rather than harshly. The Buddha also talked about the need to keep Noble Silence. When you don't have anything to say, keep quiet. That way you save your energy and you don't harm yourself or others through mindless speech."

TRY THIS:

The team speech guidelines are as follows:

- ▸ Speak only what's truthful and useful.
- ▸ Refrain from gossip.
- ▸ Refrain from unnecessary interruptions.
- ▸ Speak kindly and gently.
- ▸ Speak humbly not arrogantly.

We can all adopt these at work and in all aspects of our lives. If your speech is truthful, affectionate, useful and harmonizing, then the atmosphere you create will naturally be calm, clear and trusting.

Try following the team speech guidelines for half an hour. Speech is so habitual that it's easy to slip into wrong speech without noticing it, but if you notice you've slipped, just come back to the guidelines. If you can follow them for half an hour, why not extend that? Try following them for four hours. Then try to follow them for a day. See what difference they make to your working day.

If you're anything like us, then it's likely that you'll slip up again and again, but if you can recollect the guidelines even just three or four times in the course of a day, and make an effort to stick with them, that will begin to make an appreciable difference to the world you move in. You'll become more productive at work as your energies are more focused and the people you interact with there will be more relaxed around you and more liable to give you their trust.

## Objectivity

The Buddha placed an enormous value on simple objectivity. In the time of the Buddha there was a monk called Bahia, who lived on the west coast of India. He'd become a monk and practiced the teachings very intently without ever having seen the Buddha. But one day a great desire arose in him to go to where the Buddha was and see him. So he packed up his spare robe and begging bowl and went off on foot. It took him about a month, traveling day and night with hardly a break, to come to where the Buddha was staying.

Arriving at the Buddha's monastery, he found that the Buddha had already gone to the nearby village in order to beg his supply of food for the day. But Bahia was so keen on meeting him that he couldn't wait—he just set off in the direction indicated to find him. He hastened into the village where he saw this slow, stately figure moving very gently ahead, going from door to door, standing with his begging bowl in hand, waiting for a few morsels of rice and curry to be put into it, and then moving on to the next house.

So great was Bahia's eagerness to see the Buddha and to receive a teaching that he went straight up to him and, without waiting, without a word of introduction, he blurted out, "Lord, give me a teaching!"

The Buddha's practice was that when he was on his alms round he would never speak, he maintained absolute silence. So he said nothing and just moved on. But Bahia wasn't to be put off—he moved along behind the Buddha and repeated his request, "Lord, give me a teaching!" The Buddha took no notice. A third time, desperately now, Bahia put his request. Now another of the Buddha's rules was that if you asked him a question three times, whatever it was, however terrible the answer, he'd reply. So he just turned round and gave Bahia a direct, penetrating look and said: "In the seen, only the seen; in the heard, only the heard; in the tasted, only the tasted; in the touched, only the touched; in the thought, only the thought." Then he turned round and went on his way—and Bahia became Enlightened on the spot.

"In the seen, only the seen; in the heard, only the heard . . ." What this means is just what it says: if we want to see things as they really are we need to attend to them as they are. Just as they are. We need to be objective. But in the money arena, as in so many areas of our lives, we often find it more comfortable to leave things a little vague and not be fully objective about them.

There's a little cloud of unknowing, for example, that many of us habitually leave hanging over some items of our expenditure.

Take Betty, for example, who likes to live life in the fast lane. When she's in a rush to get to that important meeting where she needs to look good and feel in control, she'll sometimes take a cab. But Betty lives in London where transportation prices are scandalously high.

> "How much do you spend on taxis each week?" we could
>     ask her.
> "Oh, not much . . . maybe seventy-five dollars."
> "And how many rides is that?" we continue.
> "Well, at twelve dollars a ride, say six rides. That's three round
>     trips in all."
> "Hmm. And how many meetings do you have each week?"
> "Yes, okay, I get your drift okay. . . . Maybe eight or nine. At
>     twenty-four dollars a meeting, I guess that's at least two
>     hundred dollars. Ouch!"
> "And do you ever use cabs when you're running late in the
>     morning or when you're going out in the evening?"
> "Oh dear," says Betty. "You've got me. I'm going to have to
>     think again."

Few of us spend that much on our transportation needs each week but we've probably all got items of income or expenditure that we habitually over- or underestimate.

It can be very revealing first of all to make up a rough budget on the basis of what you think to be the case and then to monitor your income and expenditure for a month and take a second look. Most of us will find we make amendments in the light of actual experience. Even if you prefer not to be ruled by a budget but rather to go about spending in a more intuitive kind of way, taking the time to fill one out will leave you with a much better informed intuition. You will be clearer, more objective and more able to be honest in your financial dealings.

As well as knowing how you stand in relation to income and expenditure, it's important to know what you actually have. Many of us tend to underestimate this. The way our society is structured, with such an emphasis on the multiplication of desires, it's easy to feel that our sense of lack has a basis in objective fact. For some of us no doubt it does, but for most of us living in the West today, the realization of just how much we actually have can be a useful reminder of the material abundance we often take for granted.

TRY THIS:
Identify a few areas of spending that you habitually avoid thinking about or get stressed about or that give you unpleasant surprises (those tax bills, for instance, that you never seem to allow for).

Write down what you think you have spent, or are due to spend, on each item. Now get together with a good friend and run through your list. Ask your friend to check your thinking and assumptions and to interrogate you in much the way that we interrogated Betty in the example above.

⟲　⟲　⟲

We hope by now you will see that there is more to being truly honest than just refraining from the occasional deliberate lie. We need to make the effort to cultivate an ever-deeper authenticity, being true to ourselves and true to our deepest aspirations. In doing that, we learn to be increasingly objective in our assessments of ourselves and our situation, objective about others and their needs and objective about the world we all live in.

But those who are fully authentic—true to their deepest nature, in Buddhist terms—don't only speak the literal truth. They also make an effort always to communicate in ways that are kindly, affectionate, helpful and harmonious. In that way they help to overcome the artificial barriers we all erect to keep the world at bay. Such communication is a powerful tool for bringing about substantial positive change.

# EIGHT

# The Fifth Precept:
# Be More Aware

*Refrain from intoxication, cultivate mindfulness.*

Traditionally, the fifth precept is understood to mean abstinence, or at least moderation, in respect to drinking and taking drugs. But we can become intoxicated in many other ways as well. When we seek intoxication, however we do it, what we're essentially after is a changed mental state. We find our current state of mind unsatisfying and we try to change it. That's fine in itself. There's no problem with trying to change your mental state. But the intoxicated state is, by definition, a diminished one. It represents a loss of awareness and it can easily become habitual, even addictive.

Money plays an obvious part in the process of intoxication. You need cash to buy alcohol or drugs. But there are modes of intoxication in which money plays a more exclusive role. Shopping can be intoxicating—we can shop to distract ourselves when we're feeling bored or miserable. Gambling can be intoxicating and so can work—you can lose yourself in work in the same way that some people try to lose themselves in drink. And, of course, the process of making money itself can be intoxicating: it's easy to get high on the adrenaline buzz of business.

Before we go any further, though, it's important to be clear on one thing. We're not saying here that you should never have a drink, enjoy an afternoon's shopping, take a bet, enjoy your work and find it absorbing or get a kick from your success in business. Where these become problematic, however, is when they lead to a loss of that quality which Buddhists prize above all others—mindfulness.

"Mindfulness is the Way to the Immortal," said the Buddha, "unmindfulness the way to death. Those who are mindful do not die, whereas the unmindful are like the dead."[19] By "the Immortal," the Buddha meant Nirvana, or Enlightenment. Mindfulness leads to Enlightenment, the goal of the Buddhist life.

Buddhists use the term "mindfulness" in a very particular way which it can take a while to get the hang of. At first sight it seems as if it's not much different from the term "awareness," but mindfulness has shades of meaning that awareness doesn't fully encompass. When you are mindful you are highly concentrated, focused on what you are doing, and you are collected—poised and calm with a composure that comes from being aware of yourself and the world around you as well as being aware of your purpose.

There was a documentary series made about Buddhism for British television in the 1970s and several of our friends attribute their first interest in Buddhism to watching it. Strangely enough, what stands out above all other things for several of them, even thirty years later, is the close-up image of a pair of feet, bare on the dusty earth, pacing backward and forward, backward and forward. These were the feet of a monk going about his walking meditation in an Asian Buddhist monastery.

"That man," one of our friends said, "was unshakable. He knew exactly what his body was doing at any moment, he was fully aware

---

19. Trans. Sangharakshita, *Dhammapada* II.21. From *Dhammapada: The Way of Truth* (Birmingham, England: Windhorse Publications, 2001).

of himself and his environment. He was totally present, totally engaged. I'd never seen such composure before. I wanted to be that alive."

The monk in that film exemplified mindfulness at a very high level, achieved after years of training, but all of us have some experience of it. When you're working, for example, doing a task that you really enjoy, it's easy to become fully absorbed. Time seems to open up and expand as you become more and more involved in the present moment. Your mind grows still and calm as it focuses more and more intently on the task at hand, and you become increasingly happy and content. Few things in life are more pleasurable then the experience of mindful absorption.

Try making a practice of paying attention to your surroundings. Look for something beautiful close at hand: even half-dead geraniums in a city window box will glow with unexpected shades of red when you start to really notice them. Or there might be unnoticed glimpses to catch around your home or place of work: flashes of sunlight through the clumps of trees, the stars against the buildings at night or ants going about their business on a forgotten piece of wood. The people we rush around every day become so much more interesting as you look at them, listen to them and find out who they are. Do you know the names of everyone you encounter at work or in your neighborhood? Of course you'll never remember them all, but we could all probably make the effort to put a name to at least some of those slightly familiar faces. By paying attention, we learn to see the world with an ever-greater appreciation: as an artist sees it.

Some of the world's great artistic traditions have grown directly from the Buddhist practice of mindfulness. Zen Buddhism in Japan, for instance, gave rise to the form of poetry known as haiku. These are very short, simple poems that bring us the poet's experience of a fleeting moment, glimpsed with an extraordinary intensity of mindfulness. Each haiku is a pure snapshot of what is happening.

*Into an old well's*
*Darkness*
*Falls a camellia[20]*

Imagine camellia blossoms falling softly into darkness, where they very briefly cast echoes, fading ripples and reflections. Each instant, if we know it mindfully, is as sharply focused and evanescent as the camellia blossom floating for a moment in the well.

Stefan Zweig, an Austrian writer who lived in the first part of the last century, once visited the great French sculptor, Auguste Rodin in his studio. After some conversation, Rodin returned to his work while Zweig sat for an hour and watched him, finding himself increasingly drawn into the atmosphere of intense absorption in which Rodin worked.

"In that hour," Zweig wrote, "I grasped the secret of all art and of all earthly achievement—concentration, the rallying of all one's forces for accomplishment of one's task, large or small; the capacity to direct one's will, so often dissipated and scattered, upon one thing."

That is what we sacrifice when we give way to intoxication.

For Rodin, it seems, a high level of mindfulness was a natural gift. The rest of us have to train ourselves in it and in the course of this chapter we'll look at some of the ways you can do that, especially in relation to the ways in which you earn and spend.

We can look at the question of mindfulness in two ways. In this chapter, we will look at the practice of mindfulness of the present moment, that involves learning to give your full, undistracted attention to what is happening here and now as you go about the business of earning and spending. In the next chapter we will look at the question of mindfulness of purpose, which puts that attention into the wider context of what you are trying to do with your life,

---

20. Trans. Yuki Sawa and Edith Marcombe Shiffert, *Haiku Master Buson* (San Francisco: Heian International Publishing Company, 1978).

especially when it comes to money-related issues and your life at work.

## Mindfulness of the Present Moment

We all have different ways of experiencing a mindful engagement with the present moment. It depends on your temperament to some extent and on what brings you pleasure. Maybe you like going out into the country and connecting with the elements—the sound of running water, the feel of sunlight on your skin, the smell of autumn leaves. Or maybe you prefer going to a concert hall to hear a great pianist interpret classical compositions. Maybe there are friends whose conversation you find really engaging. Or maybe you like to cook and eat good food. We have all got different ways in which we engage our senses and our attention more deeply. When your attention is engaged in that way your mind grows calm, you become happier and you feel more fully alive. Your energies start to flow together and you become increasingly absorbed simply in what is going on. You become more focused and concentrated. That is mindfulness, and wouldn't it be great if we could naturally live our whole lives like that? According to the Buddha, all of us can. It's simply a matter of training.

Like anything worth achieving, though, it will take a certain amount of effort and commitment, especially in today's world where our lives are so fast and fragmented. There are so many demands on our attention, particularly at work where the pressures demand multi-tasking, an attempt to do several things at once that fragments our attention and leads to stress and inefficiency.

Because so much of what we do at work actively fragments our attention, if we want to be clear, focused and aware—mindful—as we go about our working lives it's necessary for most of us to do something that even more strongly draws our mind back together again. The practice of meditation can make a huge difference. That was the experience of Rosemary Tennison, who is a publishing director at Cambridge University Press, responsible for the editorial department in their Education Group, which produces books for schools.

Rosemary enjoys her work, but it hasn't always been easy.

"Publishing is a vocational task and many of us do it from love, but it can also be highly stressful. We set ourselves very high standards and it can be a struggle to achieve these. When there are deadlines to meet, you often find yourself working extra hard, putting in long hours in order to meet them. So it's easy to get stressed and lose perspective. You become unhappy and irritable, sleeplessness can set in, and you get headaches. You rush to make decisions, not standing back enough, and you find yourself worrying a lot and generally not doing the job well. When this happens, people often take it out on their families. The people you know best, the ones you can relax with, are often those you treat worst. You lose your temper at home and you get depressed. In extreme cases it can lead to long-term sickness."

Some years ago Rosemary discovered that she was suffering from high blood pressure and she was generally feeling the effects of stress. She'd been working closely with a friend and colleague but now she was being offered the chance of promotion, leaving her friend behind. Rosemary considered her position. "Do I want this promotion," she wondered, "or do I want to live my life well?" She realized that she wanted both, but the question prompted her to look more closely at her life. She had read Buddhist books before and she felt that somewhere in Buddhism she could find the tools to help her to gain some control over her mind. She was looking for a way of dealing with her stress, but also wanted to learn how to put her major life questions, such as the issue of promotion at work, into perspective.

She attended a meditation course at the Cambridge Buddhist Centre and took to it right away. Learning to meditate helped her to lower her level of stress and after a few months members of her family began to comment that she seemed to be much happier, calmer and more balanced.

Rosemary began to wonder whether others at work might benefit from meditation too, so she invited someone from the center to come and run a similar course at the press. They ran a couple of courses there and people seemed to profit from them.

"Then we asked what's going to happen to everyone once the course ends? Will they just stop meditating? So I decided to organize a regular meditation group at work."

At first the group met on their lunch hour in the company's sports and social club. Then the human resources director arranged for them to have a room of their own, which Rosemary set up as a meditation room, with attractive objects, a small Buddha statue and pictures on the wall.

Colleagues often approach Rosemary and ask about meditation, although not everyone who asks takes it up. Her boss at first found it all a little strange. When he saw the change that took place in Rosemary and others, however, he began actively to encourage her meditation group and once or twice has asked her if she could find a way to get a particular staff member to meditate.

"People comment these days on how friendly and supportive my department feels. There's generally a very high level of positivity and effectiveness in my team. I work with good people, but I think Buddhism and meditation have played a part in making that kind of atmosphere."

We've already looked at the loving-kindness meditation, one of the two practices that Rosemary's group has learned. It helps them to deal with the prickly mental states that are so easy to get into at work when deadlines are pressing. They alternate that with another practice, one that is designed more particularly to calm the mind and bring about states of heightened concentration and awareness—greater mindfulness. This practice is called the mindfulness of breathing. It was taught by the Buddha himself, and if you practice it regularly and sincerely, he said, it can lead you all the way to Enlightenment.

TRY THIS:
### THE MINDFULNESS OF BREATHING MEDITATION

You begin the practice by taking yourself off to a quiet spot where you know you won't be disturbed (put a sign on the door, switch off the phone) and set yourself a clear period during which you're going to meditate and do nothing else. You might start with ten minutes or so, then build up to twenty. Many of those who do this practice regularly sit for forty or more minutes a day, but don't be in a rush to extend the length of the practice. Just do what feels comfortable. Even five minutes spent trying to develop mindfulness each day can make a real difference to your life.

Get into whatever meditation posture suits you best, whichever will allow you to be both comfortable and alert. If you want to sit cross-legged on the floor, with your buttocks supported by a cushion or two, be sure you can do that in a way that comfortably allows your knees to touch the floor in front of you. If you can't easily do that, try kneeling astride a heap of cushions with your knees firmly on the floor and your buttocks firmly supported (some people also use a small meditation bench to sit like this). If neither of these postures works comfortably for you, try sitting in a firm chair, like a dining chair, with both feet squarely on the floor in front of you, with your back upright and your hands resting one on top of the other in your lap.

Now do a brief body-scan to set yourself up for the meditation and let go of any tension you may be carrying. Start with your feet. Bring your attention to them, maybe wriggle your toes and flex your feet a few times, and just become aware of what's going on with your feet. Let go of any tension you might find, allow your feet to relax, and then move on up to your calves. Do the same thing again, flex your calves and allow them to relax, and then let your attention go to your knees, your thighs and then your groin and buttocks, all the time letting go of any tension you discover. Allow your attention to rise up your back and thorax. Become aware of your lower back, your abdomen, your upper back and your chest. Letting go of any tension you find, become aware of your neck and throat, the back of your head and your face. Gently relax the muscles of your face and scalp.

Close your eyes or let your gaze fall, your eyes relaxed and unfocused, on a spot a few feet in front of you on the floor.

Take a few deep breaths and feel yourself relaxing into your meditation posture. You should be relaxed but upright and alert. Now you can begin the practice. What you try to do in the mindfulness of breathing practice is to become aware of your breath. Simply that and nothing more. You don't try to interfere with the process of breathing, don't make your breaths longer or shorter, just attend to the process of breathing, becoming increasingly aware of it.

In the first stage, to help keep your attention on the breath, count each breath, at the end of every out-breath. Breathe in, breathe out, and count "one." Breathe in, breathe out, and count "two" . . . and so on up to "ten." When you've done that, don't pause, just go back to "one" and so it continues, counting the out-breaths from one to ten, over and over.

In the second stage the practice becomes slightly more subtle. Rather than counting after the out-breath, you count before the in-breath, from one to ten, over and over. Count "one," breathe in, breathe out. Count "two," breathe in, breathe out. And so on up to "ten" and then back to "one" again. Again, don't try to force the breath, don't try to breathe longer, shorter or deeper. Let it proceed naturally.

In the third stage, stop counting and just watch the breath, simply attending to the process of breathing itself. Just let it flow, sit with it, and be fully attentive to it.

In the fourth and final stage, you focus your attention at that point where you first become aware of breath entering your body. Usually it's a slight tickle at the tip of the nose, but however this sensation occurs, locate it and attend fully to it as it changes with every passing moment.

If you can allow your attention to rest, happily and undistractedly, on such a subtle moment of experience for even only five minutes, then you will have become highly concentrated. Your energies will all be flowing together and you will be in a very relaxed and highly refined mental state.

Although this may sound simple, it can be a little difficult to do at first. It's quite common to find yourself counting "thirty-two, thirty-three, thirty-four . . ." having forgotten to return to one after reaching ten. And most people find that, even if they can put aside the physical discomfort of all their accumulated bodily tensions, their minds wander off on courses of their own, oblivious to any attempt to keep them focused on the breath.

There are many different methods you can employ to deal with the hindrances to meditation that are bound to occur. We looked briefly at some of these in the chapter on contentment. You might also consider taking a course at a Buddhist center where these practices are taught, for there is much you can learn from more experienced meditators. You can also get a great deal of support from sitting together with others, as the people in Rosemary's group discovered. If her experience intrigues you, you might also consider starting a sitting group with some of your colleagues at work. Buddhist meditation teachers are often happy to respond to invitations to come and teach.

## Other Ways of Practicing Mindfulness

The regular practice of meditation is an enormous help in the development of mindfulness. But it is important to extend your effort throughout your working day. The fruits of the mindfulness of breathing practice, great as they are, can soon be eroded by the daily grind. In the West today, and especially in the workplace, we're all subject to so much input. How do you keep on top of that without allowing your mind to become completely fragmented?

The essence of mindfulness is doing one thing at a time and doing it with complete attention. Some of our readers might wonder, who can do just one thing at a time when there's so much to do? There you are, typing a memo, when a colleague comes in for an urgent discussion, your phone rings, and as you reach for it you see that the fiftieth e-mail of the day (this time from your boss) has just arrived. In the meantime you're late for an appointment and you're behind on preparing the presentation you have to give tomorrow. One thing at a time? Not possible.

But, believe us, one thing at a time is the *only way* to deal effectively with a life like this. The reason it works is that it allows us to give our full attention to the task at hand. Not only that, we also give each task only as much attention as it needs and no more.

Think for a moment of a great kung fu fighter. In the film *Crouching Tiger, Hidden Dragon,* the young girl Jen, a highly trained fighter, finds herself in a tavern where, to prove herself, she provokes a fight with all the other fighters present. They come at her from all angles and in many different ways, but Jen concentrates. She deals with them one at a time and usually in very little time indeed. She gives each of them just enough of her concentrated attention to deal with them effectively, then she moves on and attends to the next attacker. Focused attention is one of the keys to Jen's success. If she'd lost her concentration—even for a moment—if her attention had become divided, she'd have been sunk.

In her work with executives and business teams, Ronna Kabatznick of MGH Consulting offers training in "Mindful Management." Mindful Management, she says, describes a state of mind that has the capacity to maintain a sense of peace, security and balance, even in the midst of chaos and change. When you make the commitment to be mindful, you are present—right here and now—which is a gift to yourself and others around you. When you listen, you listen. When you work, you work. When you're angry, you feel it and you have a choice to act on it or not. Mindfulness helps you be where you are when you're there. It is the art of conscious living and working.

Here are some suggestions for those who wish to practice mindfulness in the course of their working day, based on exercises that Ronna teaches.

1. Breathe

Before you make a telephone call, or log on to your computer or do any other type of activity, such as leaving your desk or other place of work, become aware of your breathing. Gently inhale and exhale three breaths, following the breaths closely and feeling the body sensations connected to breathing. Simply follow your breath in and out for a moment before reaching out to "do" something. Just breathe.

"Oh, c'mon!" we can imagine some readers thinking. "If we had time to breathe around here we'd have met our deadlines weeks ago!"

But think about it. Three breaths. Nine seconds. Even if you do this exercise forty times in the course of the day, that's a six-minute commitment.

The difficulty with doing this exercise is not about time. It's partly an issue of remembering to do it, which is quite demanding. But even if you only remember to do it four times in the course of the day, you will experience a significant difference. Acting more consciously, with greater awareness of what you're doing, how you're feeling and what your intention is, makes you clearer and more directed. The call you were about to make, the work you were about to do on your computer, will be that much more focused and precise.

2. Listen mindfully

During a conversation, give your full attention to the person who is talking to you. Listen closely. When you find your mind wandering, bring it back to listening. Notice how listening affects your relationship and your attitude toward the speaker.

People at Windhorse Trading remark on their CEO's capacity to give them his undivided attention in conversation. Whatever else is going on around them in their busy communal office, Vajraketu remains noticeably focused on the discussion at hand. That gives people a sense that he has really heard and understood them. They feel fully met, even if the communication only lasted a few minutes.

In the channel-hopping, quick buzz, multi-tasking culture we live and work in, we tend not to give people our full attention when they're with us. While we're speaking we're thinking all kinds of other thoughts. "What's the next task on my list? What am I going to wear tonight? Did I remember to call and book a car service? How long is it till lunch? What are we going to do if the budget doesn't work out? I'm hungry. . . ." And so on.

Some of these points may well be worth thinking about, in which case we ought to give them our more complete attention if only for a moment or two. Or perhaps they're not worth thinking about, in which case they're simply a distraction from the task at hand, possibly because we're bored and want some stimulation. But giving our full attention to another person is itself stimulating. However dull they might appear to be, the person you're with right now is a human being with a full set of human qualities that you can respond to. If you don't see those qualities in them at first, ask yourself: Am I looking deeply enough, attending closely enough?

When people feel that they have your full attention sometimes they blossom before your eyes. Even if the communication only lasts three minutes, it can make a big difference to both of your days.

Mindful listening is also more efficient. Whatever has to be communicated is communicated with the minimum of waste and the least prospect of misunderstanding. Besides making for a richer human life, it makes good business sense too.

3. Notice your bodily posture

Every day at a certain time (say 9 a.m., noon, 4 p.m. and 10 p.m.) notice what posture you're in—whether sitting, standing, lying, walking—and whether your body is comfortable or not. Ask yourself: is this an alert, relaxed posture? If not, do what you can to make it so.

The way you hold your body says a lot about what's happening in your mind. That's why we speak of a person's "body language." We can, for example, tell what's happening with them from how they walk. Do they have a confident stride or a diffident shuffle? Our states of mind are reflected in our bodies, but the process works to some extent in reverse as well—by changing what's going on in our bodies we can change our states of mind, to some extent at least.

Notice how you're sitting or lying right now. Now imagine what it would be like for your posture to be relaxed, but more alert. Now get into that relaxed, alert posture. Now look at your mental state. Do you feel more alert?

Much of the time we're not really aware of our posture and so we slump or hold ourselves rigid and defended, shamble along dispiritedly or march triumphantly; all the time communicating those states to others and sustaining them in ourselves partly by way of our posture.

By changing your posture you can have a positive effect on your mind. The first step is to have some degree of ongoing awareness of what's happening with your body. Very few people have a continuous sense of what's happening with their body, but we can all increase our extent of bodily awareness by making an effort to be more mindful. A regular check-in with our body can be a very useful start to that process.

4. Keep a "mood diary"

As well as being aware of our body, we need to become more aware of our mental states, in particular, our passing moods. Moods color the whole way in which we see the world. When we're in a happy, optimistic mood the world is bright and pleasant, life seems easy and our future full of hope. When we're in a depressed mood we wonder why anyone bothers and when we're in a frustrated mood the world is hard, spiky and resistant. But these are all moods and the world, as it is, continues, as it does, despite them.

If we want to be objective at work and deal with people and the world as they are in themselves, it's important to be aware of the distinction between the world as it is and the world as seen through the filter of our passing moods. To do that, we have first to become aware of our moods themselves. That is the purpose of the Mood Diary.

Buy a simple notebook, a small one is preferable, and as soon as you become aware of a mood—be it frustration, calm, pleasure, irritation, boredom, whatever—write it down along with the time of day. See if you can do this every day for one week. At the end of the week, review your mood diary. What do you observe about your moods? Do you have many or few moods in a day? How many moods do you experience over a week's time? Are most of them pleasant or unpleasant moods? What are the mood states that make life most difficult for you? Which ones do you find hardest to get out of? Which are the easiest to leave behind?

Following these four practices, you'll learn to become more aware of yourself, both at home and at work. They will open up the world of mindfulness for you, a world of ever-deepening awareness that will ultimately enrich every aspect of your life.

## Mindfulness at Work

Most of us spend most of our waking time at work, and the challenge that many of us face is to make our work more fully into an arena for the kind of practices that will allow us to cultivate mindfulness, truthfulness, contentment, generosity and loving-kindness.

Ruchiraketu's first contact with the Western Buddhist Order was at a Festival of Mind, Body and Spirit in London in 1978. There he came upon a flyer that contained a picture of a group of people working together. The caption read something like "Buddhists working together to build a new vegetarian café." He had been practicing meditation for a time, but the idea that you could combine meditation, spiritual practice and ordinary work really excited him, and he got involved in the Order at the London Buddhist Centre.

When he joined Windhorse Trading, the company was in its seventh year. Sales had been growing year after year, but cash flow was still very tight, profits were low and the immediate goal of the company was to repay debts. Some in the business were struggling to make sense of what they'd committed themselves to. They all had the idea that work could be a transforming spiritual practice but sometimes it didn't seem to be that way. It could seem like hard, grinding work for little apparent reward—either personally or in terms of the business. It was hard to meditate under those conditions, hard to study, and people didn't always treat each other kindly. Tempers would fray and there was an undercurrent of mild irritability in the workplace.

The company agreed that Ruchiraketu would be taken on explicitly to act as a spiritual friend to everyone involved in the business. Everyone else was caught up in the pressures of work and it was easy for them to lose the spiritual perspective on what they were meant to be doing. Ruchiraketu would keep himself clear of those kinds of tasks and instead spend his time meeting up with people, befriending them and helping them to keep in touch with the wider picture. He would be able, where necessary, to uphold the spiritual needs of the workers as opposed to the material needs of the business.

"I'd meet up with people and ask them how things were going in their lives in quite a broad way, not just in terms of their work. I'd explore their meditation and study with them, and sometimes it was necessary to remind people that there was more to life than work.

We were all living communally at that time, and the work seemed to be absorbing people to such a degree that they'd bring it home with them and there was little distinction between home and work. I'd remind people to talk about things other than business over the dinner table. Sometimes I'd get another conversation going—'Have you read any good books lately?'—that kind of thing.

"What I noticed was that when most people became totally absorbed in the business they'd be quite happy for a while, but then other neglected parts of themselves would come to the fore and they'd start to wonder why they were doing it at all. Business can be very absorbing and it can be very intoxicating. You can so easily lose sight of a wider perspective. Some few people thrive on that—I guess those are the natural entrepreneurs—but most people need to lead more balanced lives."

It wasn't always clear to Ruchiraketu how he could best help people.

"Occasionally I'd come upon people who seemed to be stuck. Either they were unhappy in their work or they weren't realizing what seemed to me to be their real potential. I wondered what I could do to help. They'd say things like 'I can't study' or 'I can't meditate' or 'I can't go out and sell things,' but I knew that they could. How could I get them to see that for themselves? How could I help them to move on? I could try to be a good friend to them, but that didn't seem to be enough. When someone was expressing self-doubt, for example, I didn't know whether it was best to challenge them on it or just to empathize with them and hear them clearly—what would help most? I hadn't a clue."

Ruchiraketu began a study of the psychology of work and workplace relationships that was to absorb him for many years. In particular, he concentrated on learning about how teams work.

"The way the business had grown, we saw that we could no longer think of ourselves as a single team working together. There wasn't enough face-to-face communication between everybody; we weren't able to transmit responsibility downward as effectively as we wanted to, and people weren't as easily able to form deep friendships with those they worked with. Friendship and responsibility both call on you to go beyond yourself for the sake of others, but you need a context that allows you to develop them.

"It's easy to say that you want to help all living beings everywhere. But that can stay an idea. But you can start on it by trying to help your close friends, trying to put their needs ahead of your own some of the time. That's a much more practical and realistic goal. So we tried to create situations at work where people were able to befriend each other. We made spaces in the teams where people met to share themselves and their lives in ways that might or might not be connected with work."

The teams might study together, or report to one another how things are going for them personally. Each week there is an hour and a half slot scheduled for that type of activity and there are short periods for checking in together at the start of each day.

"Carrying responsibility, both in terms of being responsible for getting a particular task done and in terms of being responsible for the spiritual well-being of others, is an effective means of personal development. It makes you more objective, less self-preoccupied. There's a low-level narcissism that runs like a red thread through Western society. We can be terribly self-centered, preoccupied with our own comfort and the minutiae of our passing mental states. The creation of work-teams allowed us to transmit responsibility outward. People could take responsibility for their teams, including each other's spiritual welfare, in ways they couldn't with regard to the business as a whole. We began to appoint team-leaders and in time a more structured way for people to take more responsibility began to emerge."

Ruchiraketu started attending meetings of the different teams around the business to see how they could be more effective, spiritually and materially.

"When it came to business matters, people were able to set goals and develop strategies to achieve these. But when it came to the spiritual dimension of their lives, they tended to be more vague. How could you know you were making spiritual progress? How could you measure that? What target might you set?"

The French thinker Simone Weil suggested that the spiritual life is only really lived at that crucial point which is the interface between the Ideal and the Real. By the Real we can take her to mean the mundane, the ordinary, the everyday. It is here that our ideals of spiritual practice meet resistance.

"Issues that affect people in their spiritual lives affect them in their work and vice versa. But the concrete situation of the work allows for very specific feedback. It's easy to be vague about spiritual issues when talking about them purely in the abstract. For example, pretty much everyone would like to be more kind. But when you're working in a pressured team it soon becomes clear just how kind you really are."

In their team meetings each week, Ruchiraketu encouraged people to talk about their spiritual goals and the small changes that would let them know whether they were making progress toward them or not.

"Someone packing orders in the warehouse who wanted to develop mindfulness, for instance, could review his progress by checking whether or not his level of packing mistakes was decreasing. People would get together in pairs and set targets for themselves each week to be reviewed the following week."

Working with the various teams in this way they began to integrate the spiritual and the material targets of the business more.

"Some of the salespeople, for example, were good at making appointments with customers, others weren't. We decided to try and tape them at work and see what we could all learn from that. We'd play back the tapes together, discuss them and see if they could improve their approach. Issues like self-confidence emerged. Good salesmen had it, less successful ones didn't. But self-confidence and self-esteem aren't just business issues—they're personal spiritual issues as well—and both dimensions could be addressed through the medium of work."

The issue of mindfulness at work has long been an active concern of Dr. Saki F. Santorelli, an associate director of the Stress Reduction Clinic that is the heart of the Center for Mindfulness in Medicine, Health Care and Society at the University of Massachusetts. He had seen how mindfulness plays an effective part in reducing levels of stress. He then began to look at how the practice of it could be extended into every minute of the working day, starting with what we do after getting up in the morning and continuing right up to our return home in the evening.[21]

At the heart of workday mindfulness practice, he says, is the intention to be aware of and connected to whatever is happening inside and around us, as well as the determination to initiate change when called for.

An example of this process is revealed in a story told to him by a physician friend. His friend recounted that as his clinical practice grew busier and more demanding, he began to develop minor symptoms of stress, such as neck and shoulder tension, fatigue and irritability. Initially, these symptoms disappeared after a good night's rest or a relaxing weekend. But as his practice continued to grow, they became persistent. What is more, much to his chagrin, he noticed that he was becoming a chronic clock-watcher.

One day, while attending to his normal clinical duties, he had an idea. He walked over to the office supply cabinet and pulled out a package of little green dots, the kind used for color-coding files. He put one on his watch, deciding that since he couldn't stop looking at it, he'd use the dot as a visual reminder to center himself by taking one conscious breath and dropping his shoulders.

The next day he placed a dot on the wall clock because he re-

---

21. Reproduced with permission from Claude Whitmyer (ed.), *Mindfulness and Meaningful Work: Explorations in Right Livelihood* (Berkeley: Parallax Press, 1994).

alized that if he wasn't looking at the watch on his wrist he was looking at the clock. This got him going, and by the end of the week he had placed a green dot on every exam room doorknob. Whenever he saw one, he'd pause, take a conscious breath and drop his shoulders.

A few weeks after initiating this workday practice, he discovered that, much to his own surprise, he had stopped, taken a conscious breath and relaxed his shoulders one hundred times in a single day. This simple, persistent decision to be mindful had been transformational. He felt much better. More important, his patients began telling him that he was "much more like himself." That was the icing on the cake.

We can all use what is constantly before us as a way of waking up to our innate capacity for stability and calm: that is, our capacity for mindfulness.

Dr. Santorelli once worked with a group of harried receptionists who described their reaction to the telephone ringing. It made them feel, they said, like one of Pavlov's dogs. There'd be a ring and a reaction, a ring and a reaction. He suggested instead that they try using the first ring of the telephone as a reminder to take one breath, return to themselves and only then to take the call.

For many of them, this simple practice became a powerful agent of change. Some said that people they had spoken with for years on the telephone didn't recognize their voices—they were speaking at a more measured pace and their voices had settled into the lower ranges. The telephone no longer elicited a mindless and immediate reaction from them. They had learned to respond with awareness to its sound. Through the action of mindfulness, the ring of the telephone had shifted from an object of threat and demand to a vehicle for cultivating greater awareness.

Having experimented with the "green dots" method on his own watch, Santorelli found that, like any other method, it can quickly sink into the realm of the unconscious. Pretty soon the dots can become just another part of the watch face, completely unseen, and lose their ability to help to generate awareness. No method is more than a temporary means. Our real work is in the remembering. This act of remembering, of recollecting and coming back to ourselves and to our intentions, is what we call mindfulness.

Santorelli developed a list of exercises which we've called "Twenty-one Ways to Be Mindful During the Workday." They're small, simple practices, but they have the power to radically improve the quality of your work, and your home, life.

## Twenty-one Ways to Be Mindful During the Workday

These Twenty-one Ways are simply a road map. In order to work with them successfully you need to explore and adapt them for your own circumstances and temperament. Dr. Santorelli developed them on the assumption that you drive to work and your workplace is an office, but it's not that difficult to figure out a set appropriate to other circumstances. Whatever list you finally come up with, you need to keep an open and experimental relationship to it. See what works for you and try to keep the practice alive.

1. Take between five and forty minutes in the morning to be quiet and meditate. Sit or lie down and be with yourself. Gaze out the window, listen to the sounds of nature or the city, take a slow quiet walk where you won't be too disturbed.

2. While your car is warming up, take a minute quietly paying attention to your breathing.

3. While driving, become aware of bodily tension, such as your hands wrapped tightly around the steering wheel, your shoulders raised and stomach tight. Consciously work at releasing and dissolving that tension. After all, does being tense help you to drive better? What does it feel like to relax and drive?

4. Don't play the radio or put on any music. Just be with the sounds that are going on.

5. If you do highway driving, experiment with riding in the right lane, going five miles per hour below the speed limit.

6. When stopped at a red light or toll plaza, pay attention to your breathing and to the sky, the trees or your quality of mind.

7. Once you park at the workplace, take a moment to orient yourself to your workday. Use the walk across the parking lot to step into your working life, to know where you are and where you are going.

8. While sitting at your desk or other workspace, pay attention to bodily sensations, again consciously attempt to relax and rid yourself of excess tension.

9. Use your breaks to really relax rather than simply to pause. Instead of having coffee or a cigarette, or reading, try taking a short walk or just sit quietly in your workspace, renewing yourself.

10. At lunchtime, don't stay at your workspace, instead try changing your environment.

11. If you have one, try closing your door and take some time to consciously relax.

12. Stop for one to three minutes every hour during the workday. Become aware of your breathing and bodily sensations, allowing your mind to settle. Use it as a time to regroup and recoup.

13. Use the everyday cues in your environment as reminders to "center" yourself. What can be your version of the green dots or the receptionists' telephone ring?

14. Take some time at lunch or other moments in the day to speak with some of the people you work with. Try choosing topics that are not work related.

15. Choose to eat one or two lunches every week in silence. Use the time to eat slowly and just be with yourself.

16. At the end of the workday, try retracing your day's activities, acknowledge and congratulate yourself for what you've accomplished. Then make a list *for tomorrow*. You've done enough today!

17. During the walk to your car, pay attention to your envi-

ronment. Become aware of yourself breathing the crisp or warm air, feel the cold or warmth of your body. What might happen if you opened up to these environmental conditions and bodily sensations rather than resisting them? Listen to the sounds around you. Can you walk without feeling rushed? What happens when you slow down?

18. At the end of the workday, while your car is warming up, sit quietly and consciously make the transition from work to home. Take a moment to simply *be*. Enjoy it for a moment. Like most people, you're probably heading into your next full-time job—home!

19. While driving, notice if you are rushing. What does that feel like? What could you do about it? After all, you're in control.

20. When you pull into your driveway or park on the street, take a minute to orient yourself to being with your family again or to entering your home.

21. Try changing out of your work clothes when you get home. This simple act may help you make a smoother transition into your next "role"—most days you can probably spare five minutes to do this. Greet each of your family members or the people you live with. Take a moment to look into their eyes. Try making the time to take five to ten minutes to be quiet and still. If you live alone, feel what it is like to enter the quiet space of your home, the feeling of entering your own environment.

## Cultivating Positive Mental States: The Four Right Efforts

For Vajraketu, the CEO of Windhorse Trading, work itself is a highly effective spiritual practice.

"There are times when the pressures of work can make it difficult to maintain positive mental states. It would be so easy to think: 'Hey, a Buddhist livelihood is supposed to support my spiritual practice. I'm feeling a bit tired right now. If I keep going at work, my meditation won't be so good tomorrow. I'd better go home and rest.' But if we were always to give in to thoughts like that we'd probably get nowhere, either spiritually or in terms of business. It's easy to get into states of excessive self-concern, but most people can handle a bit of tiredness and a bit of pressure so long as it doesn't go on for too long. In any situation you have your bigger purpose that goes beyond the immediate situation. If you remain connected with that purpose you can often push through passing negative mental states. Becoming more objective and more robust is part of our practice."

For most people at Windhorse Trading, Vajraketu has come to exemplify the benefits of working on the self in the context of right livelihood. For many years, he's made a practice of paying particular attention to the Buddha's teaching of "the four right efforts." These are: the effort to prevent the arising of negative mental states; the effort to eradicate negative mental states that have arisen; the effort to cultivate positive mental states and the effort to maintain and develop positive mental states that have arisen.

Vajraketu focused his efforts on the first and third of these— preventing the arising of negative mental states and cultivating positive ones.

"I sit at my desk and work, and I also interact with people who look to me for guidance at work, both in terms of the business side of things and also spiritually. Naturally they want to come and talk to me, and my impulse, if I'm interrupted in what I'm doing, is to experience irritation and impatience. But as a practicing Buddhist and as a manager, I've got to suppress that. That's the first right effort and I work with it a lot in that sort of context.

"But of course you've got to do more than just suppress negativity. In fact, the tendency to suppress irritation can close me in on myself and cut me off from people emotionally. So I have to work with the third right effort as well. I have to cultivate positivity so as to open myself up to the people who come to see me and give them my full attention. I used to find this very difficult to do but with practice and over time I've learned how to generate the necessary feelings of warmth, kindness and openness quite easily. It's almost a physical thing. I feel the difference in my chest and in my posture. I can be closed in or I can open up, and I've learned how to open up by working on it. I hardly ever give way to irritation these days and I feel a lot of genuine goodwill for the people I work with."

When he first took over running the business, Vajraketu experienced a fairly continuous level of stress. Since then, he's learned to work with his mental states much more creatively.

"At Windhorse, I've had to work on my mental states, hour by hour. I used to be passive in relation to my passing moods, but I've learned not to be so. If I find myself in a bad mood, I realize that I just can't afford that—it's a drag for me, it's bad for others and it's bad for the business—so I work to get out of it. First I make it conscious to myself. I say: 'This is just a bad mood. It isn't good enough. What am I going to do about it?' Moods always hook on to something, and if I indulged my bad moods, I could easily find myself getting irritated with someone. But I ask myself: 'Is the other person the problem here, or is it my mental state?' In most cases it's my mental state. Anyone can be a little irritating sometimes, but that only affects you if your mood lets it. When I become conscious in this way, I just drop it."

The effort that Vajraketu makes to work with his mental states in the context of his daily life is the very essence of Buddhist practice. He does so within the context of a situation that is designed to support his efforts to be mindful. Is it possible to practice like that outside of such a context? Unequivocally, the answer to this question is yes. As Norman Fischer, former co-abbot of the San Francisco Zen Center, puts it—

"When I lived in Green Gulch monastery, I would meditate in the morning, have breakfast and work. Meditate in the evening and go to bed. I'd go on retreats fairly frequently and everything that happened in the course of that kind of life was some kind of teaching. So why should that be different from somebody who gets up in the morning and sits, has breakfast, goes off to work? Why shouldn't they also practice the precepts? Why shouldn't they also practice mindfulness? Why shouldn't they also practice kindness and find a way to do that?"

The same sentiment is echoed by Les Kaye, Zen priest and author of *Zen at Work*, who teaches in Mountain View, California. Les worked at IBM for many years.

"There were all the usual work pressures at IBM—politics, bureaucracies and deadlines—all the things that go on in an organization. But what I discovered after a time was that IBM was my monastery. I started off thinking of practice just as sitting practice on a meditation cushion and didn't connect it with work, but I came to realize that your practice has to be expressed in everything you do during the day, and if what I do during the day is going to work at IBM, then that's where I have to express my practice in some way. In a monastery you think you understand how to practice because they say 'Clean this or prepare this meal or do this.' And you think, 'Oh, that's what it means to practice.' But when I went to IBM I had to ask myself, 'What's practice here?' At first it was a mystery, but then it became clearer. I came to realize that whatever I did at work, if I did it with good intention, was an expression of my spirituality. That understanding has been with me ever since. Wherever you go, whatever you do, that's it!"

## Four Dimensions of Mindfulness

You can look at the issue of mindfulness from four points of view. We can practice mindfulness with regard to ourselves, to others, to our environment and to reality. The first three are relatively simple. In practicing mindfulness in respect of ourselves we attend first of all to our immediate sense-experience—what are we currently seeing, hearing, tasting, touching and smelling? Then we consider things like our bodily posture, how we are currently sitting, standing or lying. And we pay attention to our thoughts and feelings as well as to what we are actually doing. The more we're able to do this the more alive and effective we can become.

Then there is mindfulness of others. This involves being aware of others as people in their own right, each of whom is unique. Too often we stereotype and try to fit people into the boxes of our own preconceptions. By attending closely to others, observing them and listening mindfully to what they have to say, we begin to see them more fully and in greater depth. People are the most interesting things there are in our world. Each of them is a deep mine of hidden treasures, and mindfulness on our part can help us (and sometimes help them) to bring those treasures into the light of day.

Mindfulness of our environment involves being aware of all the rich detail of the world all about us. Whether it is a grimy city street or a beautiful woodland walk, the world we move in is full of wonder and interest and the more aware we are of our environment, the more effectively we're able to function within it.

The exercises we've given above can help us to develop more mindfulness in respect of these three dimensions. Those three in turn find their culmination in the fourth dimension of mindfulness, awareness of reality, the ultimate goal of the Buddhist life.

As we discussed in the introduction to this book, we all in our different ways try to use money (as well as many other things) to make our lives complete. But it cannot because nothing can. Incompleteness, open-endedness, is the very essence of everything—ourselves included. Nothing is ever fixed and final because change and transience are the true nature of things. Everything, without exception, is impermanent. We like to think of this world as comprising things and people (ourselves included) that are somehow fixed, final and complete in themselves. But the truth is that everything is in a flux of constantly changing processes that we can never finally grasp and pin down. And since this is so, we can never find final and ultimate satisfaction from the world about us. Everything always changes and no sooner have we got the perfect house or the perfect job, then things change and we go off for another spin around the Wheel—our job circumstances change and the neighbors from hell move in next door.

Mindfulness of reality consists in attending to this fact as it constantly manifests before us. It involves attending closely to the changing nature of things and to seeing how everything in the world depends on everything else, how everything is ultimately contained in everything else: trees are made into paper, and authors, publishers, editors and booksellers work to get them to readers who read and finally discard them so that they decay and turn to earth which in turn supports trees. . . .

Because the world is constantly changing, the Buddha told us, we can never gain ultimate satisfaction from it. Full and lasting satisfaction can never come from having and owning. Instead, it comes from being open and alive, from responding with joy and concern to the very fact of change itself. Only through fearlessly and unconditionally embracing the fact of impermanence can ultimate satisfaction—Nirvana, Englightenment—be found.

For most of us, that is a long way off, but by cultivating the four dimensions of mindfulness we can draw ever nearer to it and, in the process, find ourselves leading increasingly rich and fulfilling lives.

The practice of mindfulness can guide us on a journey of discovery in which ultimately all the wealth of Enlightenment will be revealed. To stay on that journey, however, we need to cultivate and maintain a mindfulness of our purpose, for without that it is all too easy to be sidetracked and settle for less than the best. Mindfulness of purpose is therefore the theme we will turn to next.

# NINE

# Conclusion:
# Living Purposefully

Few of us—Buddhist or otherwise—would quibble with the proposition that life will be better if we find ways to be kinder, more generous, more content, honest and aware. Or that being cruel, mean, intoxicated, untruthful and blind to what's happening is a pretty unpleasant way to live. Steering our lives from what's obviously unpleasant to something better is an attractive end in itself. The previous five chapters in this book lay out the Path of Abundance, providing a number of practical navigation aids that you can use, as well as down-to-earth examples of ways in which some individuals are trying to live better.

Each of those chapters described one of the five traditional Buddhist precepts which you can apply to any aspect of life, your money-life included. Living in those ways—whether or not we become more prosperous as a result—will make us happier. We've described that as a "skillful" life, because happiness is hard-won. We need to learn the craft of living well, because, as we saw in the early chapters, the Wheel of Money—the Wheel of Life itself—is spun around by powerful forces that will cause us suffering unless we learn how to deal with them. We've described this as a "creative" life, because if we live in this way we are taking charge of our lives, mastering the forces of greed, hatred and delusion rather than reacting blindly to whatever threatens our cosmic sense of self-importance. You may well have started to realize some of the promises that we made to you in the introduction: finding more enjoyment, wisdom, confidence and imagination as you earn and spend money, treading the Path of Abundance.

But there's an even greater prize.

Earlier we discussed the ways in which any of us might habitually limit who we are. We looked at the implications of a life spent spinning around and around on the Wheel. The tragedy is not just that this is a miserable way to live. It's also an opportunity that we lose, because life can be so much more. We spoke of the contrast between a tight, enclosed, predictable, self-centered life and one that is a magical discovery of who we can be as we rise to our fullest potential.

Imagine your life as a work of art, as a unique masterpiece that you are painting—as an integral part of the world—day by day. Perhaps you have had glimpses at various times of your life of what you could be if you let the qualities that you most treasure come to flourish. It might have been a talent that an insightful teacher saw in you once upon a time and encouraged for a while. It might have to do with what those who care about you most value in you. Perhaps it's the way that you'd like to be remembered when your life comes to a close, the mark that in your dreams you'd like to leave upon the world.

But sometimes we forget those dreams.

In the Lotus Sutra, we read of the parable of the Drunkard and the Jewel. A man goes to his close friend's house one day, and there he gets drunk and falls asleep. His friend, having to leave on urgent business, leaves the man asleep but ties a priceless jewel into his clothing as a farewell present to him. When he wakes up, the man who was drunk goes off on his own travels, and comes to a distant country. Penniless, he slaves away to survive. But one day, his old friend comes across him hard at work. "Whatever are you doing," he asks, "toiling away like this just to feed yourself? I wanted you to be comfortable and happy, and when we last met, I tied a priceless jewel into your clothing. Didn't you know it was there all the time? There it is: go and exchange it and live in comfort, free from all poverty."

The Jewel is our real hidden wealth.

In fact, it is who we really are. But it can get hidden beneath the superficial layers of being, so much so that we don't know that it's there as we go about our lives, with us all the time. At times, it gets covered up by all of the anxious concerns and deeply etched habits that we develop. Many of those habits and concerns have to do, of course, with earning and spending money, because so much of our time and energy is absorbed in those processes. Finding the Jewel means coming into contact with the deepest level of our own being. The five precepts that make up the Path of Abundance are not just navigational aids to avoid suffering and live happily. They are ways to help us peel back those superficial layers of being, to peel back the constricting folds of craving and aversion, to find out who we really are and set ourselves more and more free to be so.

The parable describes the Jewel as priceless; and this is exactly what it is: beyond price, the most important thing in our lives. Our teacher, Sangharakshita, once spoke of this. "Money," he said, "isn't the most important. Success isn't the most important. Popularity isn't the most important. Knowledge isn't the most important. Culture isn't the most important. Religion isn't the most important. Meditation isn't the most important. . . . The most important thing in life, the most precious thing in the whole world, is contact with one's own true self, between the surface of one's being and its depths. This is more precious than the whole world . . . this is the priceless jewel."[22]

It's not to be sacrificed for anything.

Another reason why the Jewel is chosen as a symbol for the true self is that it cannot be soiled.

"It may lie hidden in dust and dirt for ages, but when the dirt is removed then the jewel shines and sparkles clean and bright as ever. In the same way our own true nature is essentially pure. It may be hidden for the greater part of our lives by passions of various kinds—ignorance, anger, bigotry and so on—but once those de-filements are removed, it shines in its original splendor. In truth it has not been defiled at all."[23]

Life's great adventure is discovering this jewel: helped by the five precepts that make up the Path of Abundance, it's a journey of mindfulness of our purpose. What that purpose might be is for each of us to learn. It's our own purpose, and the journey will take us in different directions. There's no one generic outcome, and we will change our lives in our own way as we uncover it. As we become more aware of our purpose, we'll find that we come to lead more and more clearly focused, committed lives, whether that commit-ment takes a Buddhist form or any other.

## Committed Lives

We have charted the unfolding of purpose in the lives of five com-mitted Buddhists—and the very different changes that they made as a result—who spoke to us while we were writing. Whether they found themselves living and working more or less among fellow Buddhists is not the point. The point is that in all these cases, there

---

22. Sangharakshita, *The Drama of Cosmic Enlightenment: Parables, Myths and Symbols of the White Lotus Sutra* (Glasgow: Windhorse Publications, 1993).
23. Ibid.

is a golden thread of purpose, albeit a purpose that is distinct for each of them. Discovering and living out your own purpose is the greatest reward for treading the Path of Abundance.

## MARC LESSER

Marc Lesser began to practice at the San Francisco Zen Center when he was twenty-one years old, during a one-year leave of absence from college. He spent the next ten years there.

During his time at the center he continually found himself being asked to do things of which he had no experience. For example, he found himself running a farming program at Green Gulch Farm for three years, where they used draft horses instead of mechanical power.

"I couldn't believe they were asking me to do that. I had absolutely no experience with farming or horses, and yet I found that I loved it. I was very much at home with those horses and I learned to weld, to repair a harness and to farm—I just loved it. Then, of course, as soon as I started feeling comfortable there, I got thrown into the kitchens at the Tassajara Retreat Center and I found I loved cooking. So I spent a year in the kitchens."

In his tenth year at Zen Center Marc was asked to be the director of Tassajara. Again he wondered, what did he know about managing a place? But he found that he enjoyed the job immensely.

"When I think of that role the image of Superman comes to mind. The Tassajara schedule started at 3:30 in the morning. Then it was meditation, study and ritual till about 8:30 in the morning. Then I'd leave the meditation hall and, just like Superman changing into Clark Kent (or vice versa), I'd take off my robes and put on the role of a businessman. I'd be on the telephone with the president of Zen Center going over budgets and working out personnel issues and capital issues, developing projects and so on—and I really enjoyed that combination."

By now he was thirty-one years old and married with one child. He began to feel that it was important to find his place in the world outside of Zen Center, and to discover some way to support himself and his family.

"Although I was still very drawn toward Buddhist practice, and wanted that to be at the center of my life, previously I had always been asked by others to do things I didn't know how to do. Now it was time for me to ask that of myself. I decided to leave Zen Center and go to business school and figure out a livelihood outside of the organization. That was really going to challenge my practice!"

The change was shocking. Marc left the quiet, monastic setting of rural Tassajara and went straight to New York City to do an MBA.

"It was like being on another planet. I saw how attached I'd become to my identity as a reputable Zen practitioner in a management role. Suddenly I was just a college dropout with no work experience that anybody could relate to. They were hard times."

With no capital, no marketable work experience and a family to support, putting in thirty hours a week at business school wasn't easy, but Marc was highly motivated. The most difficult thing, though, was living outside of a community.

"Our life at Zen Center had such a richness. You walked outside your door and there were always people you knew. We ate communally, lived very much side by side, and yet there was a lot of space. There was this tremendous respect for people's individual space. Living in a nuclear family, it takes a lot of effort to connect with people outside of work. For me, that's the hardest thing about life in twenty-first-century America."

Two years after leaving school, Marc founded a company called Brush Dance, producing wrapping papers and greeting cards made from recycled paper and designed by artists from the San Francisco Zen Center. Initially selling through a small mail-order catalogue, the company evolved over the next few years into a publisher and wholesale distributor and as it grew it added new product lines. Ownership, though, has brought new challenges.

"I feel like I have to really be myself at work, not to have some special business garb, or business state of mind, or anything like that. I keep trying just to be myself, to be fully present in the situation. Of course I come up short. There are so many ways of not being present, partly because there are so many different aspects to my working life—there are my relationships with my board of directors, my investors, customers, the artists we work with and the other employees. And these all have their own complexities."

Together with Norman Fischer, Marc runs a group called the Right Livelihood Business Network, bringing together business managers and leaders who have some sense of spiritual practice in their work.

"It's a huge issue for many people, because there's such an emphasis on money in our culture right now. It's almost overwhelming. This is a way to recognize the power that has and to balance it by sitting or studying together."

One of the things that surprised Marc in their workshops was that a lot of people felt that they couldn't speak openly in their businesses.

"They can't express their values or even say what they see, in terms of what is or isn't being done well in their business. They don't feel that there's room for openness and honesty. But in the light of the values that I try to live by, at Brush Dance we encourage people to speak out—about their doubts, their questions and issues and about how things could work better. Given the structure we have, people often feel that it's hard to speak their truth. I tell them 'Don't go home and tell your spouse how crappy things were at work today and how dumb your boss was—come and tell me instead.' Sometimes people do, sometimes they don't."

## Sudhana

Sudhana was into making money from a very young age. He grew up in a typical hard-working English family. Before he reached his teens he was doing morning and evening newspaper rounds, washing cars and singing—for a fee—in the local church choir at weddings. He left high school at age fifteen, and trained as an electrical apprentice. It was tedious, badly paid work. He earned five pounds weekly. Even in 1967 that wasn't much. He went on to work in London as a law-firm clerk and jewelry store assistant, and then left home to travel the country as a short-order cook, waiter and gardener.

"Like many young people, I found my background dull, and dropped out as far as I could. Eventually I was living on a remote English island with my girlfriend. We got married and had a son, but we were both very much into exploring an alternative lifestyle."

Buddhism inspired him from the time he was sixteen, and when his six-year marriage came to an end in the late 1970s he moved into a residential Buddhist community that operated on the economic basis of minimal sufficiency.

"We shared everything. We meditated together morning and evening, ate together and pooled any savings that we had as a common purse. We worked together too: setting up a home moving business, Raft Removals, which kept us fed and housed at a very, very basic level and contributed a little money toward the cost of building the Buddhist center. We just focused on what we saw as the spiritual side of things. Economics meant give what you can, take what you need."

Aspects of this he loved.

"It was an adventure. We were exploring renunciation, seeing what it was like not having anything of your own."

But there was another side to it.

"Sometimes nobody really took responsibility for our shared property or the money decisions that we needed to take, and I had a sense of powerlessness in just not being able to pay for things."

At times he found this frustrating. The frustration, however, stirred in him a growing awareness of the need to be more aware of money and to deal with it more responsibly. There was a increasing awareness that he himself could and should take on more responsibility, and that taking on responsibilities through work was an important aspect of the spiritual life.

There are many Buddhist stories of spiritual apprentices who discover what they have to do only when they encounter frustration, sometimes the frustration of an irksome task set for them by their teacher. Tibetan Buddhists tell the story of Marpa, a teacher who gave his disciple Milarepa the enormously frustrating job of building a series of stone towers and then demolishing them. The sheer frustration gave birth to Milarepa's vision of what he really wanted to do. We don't, by the way, recommend deliberately designing frustration into everybody's life. But if you encounter it, and don't run away from it, then it may help to prompt a dawning sense of who you want to be—or at least of who you don't want to be—before you move on to life's next task.

From the very beginning of his Buddhist involvement, way back in his mid-teens, Milarepa was the hero who had most inspired Sudhana.

It was becoming clear to him that one of his larger life challenges would be to work with the tension between his desire for both freedom and responsibility. For him, becoming authentic would mean finding a way to reconcile those two apparent opposites.

After a short period of time with Raft Removals and work in a gardening center, Sudhana set up another cooperative venture. He wanted to get it right, and so Friends Gardening, which he founded, drew on his own experience of frustration as well as his skills as a gardener. He soon discovered that he had other skills as well.

"Most of the people who joined us preferred not to take responsibility for our decisions about money. So it fell to me and one or two friends to look after that side of things as the guys who'd got it going." They had to be aware of the economic, as well as the spiritual, aspects of Friends Gardening. "Otherwise it would have just fallen apart."

Sudhana's role involved getting sometimes unworldly Buddhists trained in landscaping and tree surgery and, of course, it involved winning business.

"Hard as it was, we trained ourselves to become really professional. Clients had great things to say about us." Soon they were winning local government contracts to maintain public spaces like hospital gardens around London. "It may sound obvious looking back on it, but those contracts would have killed us if we hadn't taken the trouble to really understand our costs and set our prices on a proper commercial basis."

For Sudhana, the task of managing Friends Gardening was in part an education in economic awareness and a discovery of his own ability to lead and develop others.

His Buddhist life, however, had by no means been just a story of work, subsistence living and meditation. His Buddhist friends and teacher gave him great encouragement to extend his awareness to the world of art, poetry, great novels and the broader world of culture. He became more and more aware of his own capacity to imagine and learn. The business and the context of community living and Buddhist center involvement that went with it provided him with an extraordinarily valuable opportunity. Those he worked with were not there just to do a job, but to share in and encourage a process of self-discovery in each other. Reflecting on this period, Sudhana is very clear that had he remained in the setting of his childhood and early youth, doing a conventional job just for pay, he would never have had the chance to open out his mind.

He left Friends Gardening in 1986 to embark on the task of resuming the education that had ended in his mid-teens. There was government scholarship aid, but this was a tough project that sometimes involved demanding part-time work alongside seven years of rigorous study. In his mid-thirties, he got his high-school diploma, then took an undergraduate degree at London University and finally completed an advanced social work qualification with a master's degree at England's prestigious London School of Economics.

Alongside this difficult achievement, he remained consistently committed to teaching Buddhism and acting as trustee for his local Buddhist center.

Sudhana is now a specialist social worker in cancer care. This is one of the ways in which he now expresses his Buddhist ideals, and it also gives him a significantly higher income than he enjoyed as a full-time Buddhist cooperative member.

"What was it like when you started to earn a middle-class salary?" we asked him. Sudhana chuckled. "The first thing I did was to buy a good Swiss watch." That was his token of financial independence, but he still lives simply in a former government housing project, which gives him the chance to save for his old age: taking responsibility for his own care is very important to him. Being relatively well paid in a flexible work environment also allows him to care for his own parents: a commitment that he takes very seriously indeed. As their situation deteriorates and requires more of his time, Sudhana often recalls the Buddha telling his followers that their first duty is to their mother and father. Should you get to know him, if you're like us, you'll be moved by his many examples of kindness and generosity in times of plenty and poverty alike.

There are several layers of meaning to Sudhana's story. Superficially, it is the story of an average English youngster who was drawn to escape the limitations of his background, who did a stint as a full-time Buddhist worker and then went on to improve his circumstances with a professional job. The richer telling is a story of growing awareness, born of both encouragement and frustration, of what he could become. There is here a consistent theme of someone striving with great effort to integrate the apparently spiritual and apparently worldly—freedom and responsibility—into a whole, authentic life.

## KARUNADEVI

Karunadevi is one of the founders of the San Francisco Buddhist Center. Until recently, she was also the executive director of a health center for teenagers in Daly City, just south of San Francisco.

As an educator working with teenagers in the late 1980s, she saw kids dropping out of school and getting involved in crime. It became clear to her that some adolescents were falling through the cracks in the service and support systems that were available to them.

"There was a lot of teen pregnancy, substance abuse, sexually transmitted disease, and those kinds of things were medical as well as social and mental health issues. We surveyed the needs of the local Latino and Asian teens, and it showed overwhelmingly that there was a great need for medical services. They weren't even getting physical exams. Some hadn't seen a doctor at all since coming to this country."

Karunadevi decided to found a health center to meet these needs. By the time they opened their doors in 1990 they had raised $175,000 and were able to employ four people, two of them part-time. But the needs they were faced with every day showed how much more had to be done. Ten years later the center had a staff of thirty and an annual turnover of more than a million dollars. As executive director doing a highly demanding job, Karunadevi faced an ever-increasing workload.

While founding the health center, Karunadevi also began to host Buddhist meditation and study groups in her living room. They grew and developed, and in due course she and a few friends began to concentrate their energies on setting up a center for the Friends of the Western Buddhist Order in San Francisco. They found and bought the premises of the current San Francisco Buddhist Center in the Mission District, and Karunadevi taught classes on meditation and Buddhism there on a regular basis.

Karunadevi got a lot of joy and inspiration from that teaching and a great deal of satisfaction from the service aspect of her work at the health center, but her own life started becoming increasingly stressful.

"At first the two activities fed each other and I was happy and able to do both. But as both organizations grew, that changed. They were still complementary in many ways, but I was just having to work too hard, and when I got to be fifty my body started giving way as well."

On the fifth anniversary of her ordination into the Western Buddhist Order, Karunadevi decided she'd have to quit working at the health center.

"I had constant symptoms of fatigue. I was writing in my journal about how I was feeling and what I was doing with my life, and realized it was the anniversary of my ordination. I thought, oh . . . okay, I'm going to tell them that I'm leaving. That'll be a good a way of celebrating my anniversary!"

Leaving the health center was a great relief.

"I'll never forget the first morning after I left. I woke up really early and my day stretched out in front of me. I had time to meditate, I planned to do some study and I had a few errands to do, but the day felt so spacious. I felt really light and energetic for the first time in years. I signed up for a watercolor class that was going to be starting in a couple of days and I was really looking forward to it. I never thought that I would do anything like that . . . it was just a whim, but I saw this class was being offered and now I could do things like that."

Seeing through her decision to leave, however, hadn't been at all easy.

"From the moment of handing in my notice there was resistance. Just watching myself as I talked with others about it, I saw how my mind constantly balked at the thought of leaving. I could go so far with thinking or talking about it and then some resistance would come up and I'd hear these voices saying 'This is premature, you're making a mistake.' I had doubts about my own finances, about the security of the health center, about whether I was going to miss that opportunity for service. And would the health center survive? It had given so much to the community."

She had some savings, but they weren't going to last forever. Friends kept telling her that she should just take some time off, give herself a long break and then get back to full-time work.

"People were asking me what I was going to do next. They said, 'Well, when you're ready give me a call.' There were projects out there waiting for me, but I didn't think that I could go down that route anymore. I needed to quit for the sake of my health, but I also needed a lot of space to just allow things to bubble up to the surface of my mind. I found myself trying to think it all through—I could do this, that or the other—but I also felt a strong resistance to all that. I could so easily have gotten myself into another stressful full-time working situation, but I knew that just wasn't right anymore. I'd always thought I'd like to devote myself fully to Buddhist work. For years I'd had a vision of doing that, but when it came to it I knew that wasn't going to support me financially. The conflict and the resistance to change were really strong and went on for some time. The voices speaking against my move were really insistent!"

But Karunadevi kept going. She thought her position through, worked out how much money she needed to live on in a year and looked at how she could cut back. Her daughter had finished college, and that helped. Today she's able to get by on just fourteen hours of paid consulting work each week and she's realized her dream of putting most of her energy into Buddhist work.

Where did she find the clarity that helped her overcome her anxiety about leaving work and ignore all the voices that told her the decision was premature?

"My spiritual friends were really helpful. They were the only people that I could sit down with and say this is what's been coming up for me this week. They gave me so much support and I knew they understood the process I was going through. They encouraged me to keep going in my chosen direction—they knew that I had a vision that was going to work out.

"Then there was meditation. It helped to calm my mind, calm all those conflicting voices, and it enabled me to confront them. Going deeper and deeper into myself somehow let the voices just fade out.

"I was driving to work one morning and I heard this voice saying 'There are parts of you that are hidden.' It popped up out of nowhere and I thought, yes—that's what I'm seeking! I want to know what those parts are. I want to know what's hidden there, and the only way to do that is to give it space and allow it to emerge."

TONY GRANTHAM

An ordained Buddhist, until his recent retirement Tony Grantham was a detective sergeant in the British police and his long police career has been intertwined over many years with his commitment to practice a Buddhist life.

There was always a current of idealism flowing through his work.

"I joined the police service on my nineteenth birthday. I felt a sense of vocation and wanted to be of service to the community. Also, being part of a structured organization appealed to me. I loved it."

After a few years as a young police officer in England, he felt the urge to travel and experience a different culture, but he wanted to stay with his career. Hong Kong was then a British colony, and he transferred to its local police department. It was a great opportunity. He worked hard, did well and took on responsibilities. Looking back, Tony says it is now clear that this was also when he became a Buddhist. He had taken a meditation course run by the TM movement in 1973 and one day, while he was meditating, he found himself overwhelmed by an extraordinary experience.

"It was a shock, really. I had this realization that there is no difference between any of us, that we all share some kind of unity. Love is the only word I can put to it, the driving force of our being."

He went on to read widely about Eastern philosophy and stumbled across one of the great Buddhist texts, the Heart Sutra.

"It rooted me to the spot. I felt that the Buddhists had got it, definitely."

But there were some difficult consequences. Like most of the other Western young men he knew in Hong Kong at that time, he was leading a rather dissolute life, chasing girls and hitting the bars every evening. The lifestyle did not fit with the experiences that he was coming to value as he meditated, nor with the ideals that were becoming ever more clear as he explored Buddhism.

"It came as a bit of a shock to me to realize how true and substantial were the Buddha's teachings and how being a member of the colonial European society there made it difficult for me to live in accordance with ethical precepts."

He felt increasingly uncomfortable with the way in which Europeans were treating the Chinese community. Few Westerners bothered to learn the language. They lived in separate enclaves. In the 1970s, Hong Kong was a notoriously corrupt society. Tony felt he had to make a change. He had to confront the Buddhist precept of honesty and its implications for how he lived and worked. At the same time, he was determined not to give up his career commitment but rather to remain true to the ideals that had drawn him into it. He returned to police work in England, where he felt that the conditions were right for him both to do the job he loved and to pursue his Buddhist calling. He got married and in due course he and his wife had three children.

For someone with a passion for engaging with people, police work presents many opportunities. Much of the work involves helping people in times of pain and crisis and preventing harm from being done, rather than depriving wrongdoers of their freedom.

"And even when you have to do that, you don't have to throw them in a cell and slam the door on them, not unless they're really dangerous. Someone who's been arrested will usually be afraid and confused, and it's important to be aware of this. I like to explain why we have to lock them up, perhaps while I'm sitting down with them on the bench in the cell. You can nearly always close the door gently, talk to them for a few minutes through the hatch, bring them a cup of tea."

There are of course times when the people police interact with are insulting and physically aggressive.

"You have be very aware of what's happening so that you can deal with a dangerous situation immediately. But you also have to stay centered and calm, and remember that these people are going through bad times. It's not personal. It's not that they hate you for yourself. You're just a target as an authority figure. We have to stay aware of this to do our job well. What was really important was for me and my colleagues to deal with people in a fair, kind and non-vengeful way whatever the situation, and to help them as much as I could along the way. That meant bearing always in mind that, like me, these were thinking, feeling beings who are also subject to suffering and hoping for an end to their suffering."

Maintaining that kind of awareness can be very challenging. Once, a six-year-old boy ran out into the road in the path of a truck and was killed. Tony was on the spot, called for police assistance and followed the ambulance to hospital. The parents did not know that their boy had been killed and the body was badly mangled and bloody. It was a very busy time at the hospital, so much so that the nurses were unable to do anything before the child's parents arrived. Tony felt he just couldn't let them see the body in that condition. He washed and laid out the corpse and combed the dead boy's hair. The parents, when they reached the hospital soon after, were torn apart by grief and anger, and their rage was directed at Tony. For some months after, the boy's mother avoided him in the street when they passed each other on his patrol route.

"That hurt. But it wasn't about me: it was just rage."

In Britain, the police are still respected by most of the community but face growing unpopularity and Tony feels that there is a common assumption among some of the general public that police officers are set apart from society. A lot of people feel that it's best not to engage with them if at all possible. Tony puts this down to a number of causes. There can, for instance, be dislike and mistrust of authority.

"The media tend to portray us as hard-bitten cynics who behave in brutish and inconsiderate ways. But many people also have a vague fear that their minor indiscretions will be found out. We can induce low-level feelings of guilt just by being around."

Sometimes, Tony has had to meet this in the Buddhist community.

"When it became known that I was a serving police officer, people's reactions in the Buddhist center ranged between the extremes of mild and supportive curiosity to shock, perhaps even outrage and disbelief. Even now, occasionally, members of my Buddhism and meditation classes ask me how I could be both a policeman and a Buddhist. I usually tell them that I just do it!"

His teacher advised him simply to be a very good policeman.

Tony believes that a key to this is to avoid compartmentalizing his life, just being himself wherever he is—with his family, in the police canteen or at the Buddhism class. He is aware that the police force can be like a closed club, cut off from the rest of society. He sees that some Buddhists too live in a separate enclave, having little to do with those who do not follow the same calling. His passionate desire to engage with people means that living in a club or enclave has no appeal.

Reflecting on the precepts helped Tony stay true to his Buddhist principles, although not all the people he met who called themselves Buddhists seemed to do that. Once, when he was a member of the Criminal Investigation Department for a small English town, he had arrested a young woman for shoplifting, and then took her back to her home to search for stolen property, which shoplifters often hoard. In her hall, he saw two Tibetan Buddhist wall hangings, and within her apartment were many other Buddhist images and statuettes. He asked what they were.

"I'm a Buddhist," she replied. "And that's nothing to do with you."

"I'm also a Buddhist," said Tony.

She got very angry. "No you're not. You're a pig. Pigs can't be Buddhists."

Tony stayed calm. "You clearly have problems," he said, "and I'd like to help you as well as do my duty. I am a Buddhist, and as you are too I'm entitled to ask you about your practice of the precepts. Are you aware of the second precept, that we do not take what has not been freely given?" Subsequently, the woman was convicted and punished with a small fine. She did not become friends with Tony, but he believes that she will always remember that encounter, as if a mirror had been held up to her face in which she could see herself with clarity.

The first precept is not to take life. Usually, in Britain, police officers do not carry guns, but Tony was asked to join a Regional Crime Squad. This was an exciting career opportunity, targeting major criminals, gathering intelligence undercover and making arrests, sometimes in very dangerous conditions.

"Great to have you with us!" said the unit commander. "We'll get you on firearms training right away."

Tony wouldn't carry a gun, and felt really sorry that he'd almost certainly lose this promotion. He had hated being required to carry a firearm when he was on the Hong Kong police force. Handing back his gun when he left had been a great relief. He said that he would completely understand if his refusal to carry lethal weapons meant that he had to give up his place on the Squad.

"We can work around that," said the commander. "No problem."

Tony was surprised and happy, particularly because he had gained the courage to be true to his Buddhist convictions in the police environment.

Before he left the police force on reaching retirement age two years ago, he was finding that more and more of his colleagues were aware of his Buddhist practice. Many congratulated him.

"Of course," he laughed, "they were quick to point out any of my own breaches of the Buddhist precepts."

Tony's oldest son, who is now twenty-two, joined the police two years ago, just as his father retired.

"I was a bit ambivalent about this as the police is a dangerous and unpopular profession. I told him that he had to really want to do it, not just follow in my footsteps. It's already been very hard for him. He had to deal with a murder in which he knew the victim. He was first on the scene. The suspects were still in the room and this guy was dead in a sleeping bag with half his head missing."

He needs his father's support when he has to deal with terrible situations of this kind. Nonetheless, Tony believes that his son is doing well in the police force.

"I told him that I'm proud of him. He has my kind of attitude. He does all sorts of kind acts that he never tells anyone about. He often talks about the goodness in the people he comes across. But he's got my hunter's instinct too, and he's keen to put the handcuffs on those who need them.

"It's quite simple really. Police officers should do their job in an impartial and fair way, bearing in mind the rights and duties of the individual and society and without fear or favor. That is the gist of the oath that every officer takes at the start of their career. Most officers manage to do all that, sometimes under extremely difficult and dangerous circumstances. I believe that I did. I certainly tried to and I admire the restraint and kindness that I so often saw amongst my colleagues.

"You don't have to be a Buddhist to be a good police officer, but if you are, it helps!"

## MARY NAYLOR

Mary Naylor is a midwife, working in the obstetrics department of a hospital in Cambridge, England. After leaving school, she took a degree in history and sociology and spent some time wondering just what she wanted to do with her life.

"I was drifting and very unclear about what direction to take, but my family conditioning and life experience thus far directed me toward work in the caring field."

She was involved in the women's movement, but apart from that she had no clear direction. A friend who was training to be a doctor invited her to visit Bangladesh and help out on a voluntary health project. She was deeply moved by what she encountered there—the poverty of the people, the way the bare facts of life and death were so much more present than they are in the West.

"My own experience of suffering was of an emotional and psychological origin. In Bangladesh I was shaken up by the example of people dedicating their lives to radical social change and to saving others from suffering and death."

It also seemed to her that there was a connection between the wealth of the developed world and the poverty of the developing world and she got interested in social justice issues. She returned to England with the intention of involving herself in campaigns relating to health in the developing world. To be effective and authentic in that, however, she saw that she'd need to have some kind of professional qualification. She decided to train as a midwife.

The word "midwife" comes from the Anglo-Saxon, where it means "a woman who is with another."

"That describes a large part of what we do. We're there to 'be with' women as they go through this momentous process, and because the process is so all-embracing, so significant for them and so dramatic, to really be there with them as they go through it is very demanding. It calls for high levels of empathy as well as clear thinking and objectivity. In fact, what I've learned is that you can't be fully objective in the situation without being empathetic, and you can't be effectively empathetic if you lose your objectivity."

The process of labor goes through a number of stages, and the job of the midwife and other assistants is to recognize what's normal and what deviates from the normal process of labor—both from the mother's and the child's point-of-view.

"You've got to be able to support the mother as she goes through the different stages and stand ready to intervene, either in her interests or the child's, should that be necessary. The different stages of labor are a given, they're the objective, physical aspect of the process. But then there's another dimension as well. The mothers-to-be bring with them all of their history, all the complexity of their lives and relationships, to this process. Everything that's meaningful to them coheres around this moment. It's so crucial, so significant, and at first they hold it all together. But as the pain builds and builds there comes a point where all of that falls away. Their bodies go through this rapid, dramatic, often terrifying change. At times it can feel as if everything's just stripped away from them, and they may feel they're going to die. It's a very acute, very raw experience, and there's no escaping it—the only way out is through it. Almost invariably, there comes a point in that process where they'll look to me, as the midwife, the person who knows and understands what's happening, and I have to be there for them—fully with it, fully present, completely supportive and yet ready and able to intervene at any moment should the needs of the child or the mother require it.

"Their first baby is one of the strongest experiences most women will face up to that point. The fathers-to-be are often present as well and they don't have an easy time of it either. There comes a point where all they can do is look on helplessly, and that can challenge their identity. There are all these complex, intense dynamics that the couple bring with them that you have to be alive to, and you don't have much time to pick them up. Then you have your own prejudices and expectations that can get in the way. You've got to be fully mindful and attentive to the situation as it unfolds, allowing the parents to go through their journey without getting in the way but at the same time being fully there to support them, ready to take a lead, give advice or intervene if necessary."

It calls on all her resources of mindfulness and empathy to be effective in these situations.

"For each woman this moment is absolutely life-changing. But for us professionals it's different. We can grow insensitive—we can be tired, we can feel overstretched and irritated, the dynamics in the room can be difficult. Then we've got our own lives going on, quite separately, as well. The challenge for me is to put my subjective responses and the objective demands of my own life aside, and just be there for the mother-to-be.

"How I am, in myself, will definitely affect the way the situation unfolds, but I can't just ignore my own life and be there as a kind of blank, purely objective presence. The mothers' senses are so heightened at that point that they'd spot that in a moment. It's not what they want and it's not what they need. They need me to be fully present: to respect them as individuals, to be competent, confident, and at the same time kind, patient and responsive. It's a lot to do with inspiring confidence that they can do it and be all right."

She didn't feel able to rise to that challenge at first.

"I just wasn't ready for it. I often had a sense of the immensity of the human experience involved and I felt overwhelmed by it. I didn't have the resources to do the job without burning out again and again."

She decided to take a break from nursing for a while. During her training in London she had met a woman who impressed her, both with her practical competence and her capacity to relate to others. She asked her how she managed so effectively to hold it all together, and her friend told her about meditation and introduced her to the London Buddhist Centre. Mary found herself increasingly drawn to Buddhist practices, eventually joining the Western Buddhist Order where she was given the name Vajrasamaya. By then she had returned to midwifery.

"My Buddhist practice helped me to experience the relationship between empathy and objectivity. Negative mental states stop one from getting anywhere near the truth of any situation one is in. In a way, maybe one could say that's the very beginning of an understanding, in the practical terms of one's life, of the Buddha's example of complete wisdom and compassion. Before I got involved in Buddhist practice I only had a *desire* for clarity and purpose. Now I've got a range of practices at my disposal that help me to *be* more clear and purposeful, more effective. The work on myself is ongoing, but I feel much more up to the task than I did before. What is more, since I was away from it, the profession, at least in England, has changed quite a lot. Now there's much more emphasis on taking responsibility for your own professional conduct and your professional development. The models being used are much more reflective, and we're expected to be much more self-aware."

The professional codes of conduct she and others work with ensure certain standards of practice and behavior.

"The Buddha's precepts are practices for the whole of life, and good professional conduct is a reflection of those principles applied. The precepts are about transforming negative states of mind and generating kindness, patience, generosity and clear thinking— that makes for good professional conduct.

"You can't do this job meaningfully without attending to your own self-development, however you see that. You've also got to put quite a bit of emphasis on the business of looking after yourself, of making sure that the important things in your life are in place. I have to take myself into consideration and make sure that my life is structured in such a way that it supports me so that I can bring the necessary sensitivity and objectivity to bear on my work. It's not that midwifery is the center of my existence, but when I'm there

I've got to be able to be fully with the women in labor. That's what it's all about."

What resources does she draw on to enable her to do this?

"Meditation and reflecting on my experience are the most important practices for me. In meditation I'm able to be more fully with myself. I know my bad habits: I can be irritable and impatient. At times I just want to be somewhere else, anywhere else almost, rather than where I am. I can be too perfectionist . . . the list goes on. But I can work on all these things in meditation. I make an effort to become more steady, present and objective. It also gives me ways of standing back and reflecting on what's going on, and I use that capacity when I reflect on my work. I think back over a delivery and I ask myself: how did that go? How was she? How was I? Is there anything there that I don't want to look at? Is there anything I'm really pleased with? Is there anything I want to follow up by way of gaining new knowledge? Is there anything I want to follow up with my colleagues? I ask myself how I was in terms of working with anxiety and impatience. I wonder how I was in relation to the precepts—was I kind, was I truthful, was I as aware as I could have been?

"I feel so fortunate to have encountered the Buddha's teachings. Without them I'd be struggling so hard with my desire to do something of value in my work, but to do it in a sustainable way. I'm sure I'd be a heavy drinker, or else on antidepressants. My own history means I don't easily have a happy life. Some of my idealism has come from a projection of my own personal unhappiness onto the world. I've had to learn to really look at myself, to face my own suffering and learn how to be happy on a more realistic basis. It's important that I don't come to the work from a sense of inner emptiness, from a sense of lack or being hard done by. Loving-kindness, mindfulness, ethics—these practices are all about experiencing the fullness of life that is mine and everybody's. If I don't keep faithful to them then I get irritable and come to the end of my tether, falling into old, unresourceful habits. But the teachings and practices are always there to come back to—it's all work in progress."

## AND YOU?

These are five different stories of the discovery and mindfulness of purpose, in which the layers that cover the hidden jewels are progressively peeled away as their authors tread the Path of Abundance. In each case, relationships to money and work have been central aspects of those stories. Those relationships can constrict us, like the dirty clothing that hid the priceless jewel in the Lotus Sutra parable. Or we can design them so that they become the stage on which we enact our own drama of discovery.

The choice is ours.

We leave you with the words of the Japanese poet Buson, who wrote the haiku that you saw in the last chapter. It's a word of encouragement and warning for us to get and spend in ways that help us find what we really, truly want—in the very deepest part of ourselves—which is so often covered up by our more superficial fears and desires.

> What you want to acquire, you should dare to acquire by any
> means. What you want to see, even though it is with difficulty,
> you should see. You should not let it pass, thinking there will
> be another chance to see it or to acquire it. It is quite unusual
> to have a second chance to materialize your desire.[24]

---

24. Yosa Buson, "New Flower Picking," quoted in *Haiku Master Buson*, translated by Yuki Sawa and Edith Marcombe Shiffert (San Francisco: Heian International Publishing Company, 1978).

# Appendix:
# Following Up

What to do next? If you would like to put more of the lessons into practice you could attend a *Mindfulness and Money* workshop led by experienced Buddhist trainers. Learn how to make money cost less of your life, how to increase your hidden wealth and craft an action plan to master money in your life. Find out more at the websites www.mindfulnessandmoney.com and www.mindfulnessandmoney.co.uk; both give details of the workshops that are run in the United States and Britain.

www.fwbo.org is the home page of the Friends of the Western Buddhist Order, the organization to which both authors belong. The site lists around eighty Buddhist centers worldwide where the main meditations mentioned in this book can be learned in more depth. The centers also offer regular classes in Buddhism (including Buddhist ethics), as well as retreats. This website also gives a list of useful links to various Buddhist sites on the Web.

www.abhayagiri.org is the home page of Ajahn Amaro's monastery, which also provides a set of links for anyone wishing to follow up an interest in Theravada Buddhism.

www.thubtenchodron.org is Bhikshuni Thubten Chodron's home page, and includes a wide range of links to Tibetan Buddhist sites among other information. It also gives updates on the inter-denominational Buddhist monastery she is in the process of co-founding.

www.everydayzen.org is the home page of the Everyday Zen Foundation that Norman Fischer has established. It contains details of Norman's teachings and schedules.

For a list of links to other Zen-related sites go to the home page of the San Francisco Zen Center, www.sfzc.org.

# Index

## About the Authors

Kulanada (Michael Chaskalson) is the founder of Windhorse Trading, a multimillion-dollar Right Livelihood business, and the author of four previous books on Buddhism. He teaches at numerous Buddhist centers. Dominic Houlder (Mahaprabha) teaches at both the London Business School and the West London Buddhist Centre, and is the founder of a successful consulting firm. Both the authors live in the United Kingdom.